MAKE THE MOST OF YOUR RETIREMENT

MAKE THE MOST OF YOUR
RETIREMENT

MIKE MOGANO

Need2Know

LIVE YOUR NEW LIFE TO THE FULL

© Mike Mogano 1996

Cover design by Joanne Readshaw
First published by Need2Know 1996
This edition published by Need2Know 1998
Need2Know, 1-2 Wainman Road, Woodston,
Peterborough PE2 7BU

All rights reserved
Edited by Anne Sandys
Typesetting by Forward Press Ltd

Contents

Introduction

1 Getting Yourself Unorganised   10

You've got it made
An unnatural state
Taking charge
Where to live
Getting more information

2 Recalculating Your Finances   27

Income
Budgeting
Taxation
Seeking advice

3 Family And Friends   47

The two of you
Enjoying grandchildren
Acting as carer
Friends
Keeping in touch

4 Looking After Your Health   62

Practise preventive healthcare
Exercise
Watch for wear and tear...
Some possible problems

5 Eating For Health   83

Eat to lose weight
Foods you can eat more of
Foods to avoid
What we drink
More about weight loss
Food supplements
Eating abroad
Summing up

6 Finding Fresh Interests   101

Back to work
Hobbies and interests

7 Helping In The Community   117

Suit yourself
A world of choice

8 It's A Computer World   130

Choosing what's right for you
Printers
Software
Add-ons
The Internet
Ten golden rules

9 Taking A Break - Or Two! 140

Holidays, holidays . . .
Especially for singles
For those with a handicap
Health and insurance
Securing your home

10 Looking Back - And Looking Ahead 158

Keeping records
Family trees
Making a will
Gifts to others
Dealing with funerals
New projects
Repartnering
Getting help in difficult times
And finally . . .

Help List 175

Index 200

Introduction

Everyone should find something of interest to them in this book.

Primarily it is aimed at those shortly to retire who want to ensure they are properly prepared for the years ahead. Secondly it is for those who have already retired and who wish to make even more of the best years of their lives. And thirdly it is for their children and grandchildren, to help them understand the traumatic changes their fathers, mothers, grandfathers or grandmothers are going through. They may even wish to buy the book as a gift for them!

What it aims to do is help enrich the lives of this country's ten million or so pensioners, many of them forced into early retirement without the benefit of long-term planning. It will guide them along a path with clearly labelled signposts such as 'Getting Unorganised', 'Recalculating Your Finances', 'Finding Fresh Interests', 'Looking After Your Health' and 'Family and Friends'.

It also covers holidays, healthy eating, ways of helping others within your own community, some computer basics and ways to capture memories for your loved ones to cherish for years to come.

Each topic has been carefully selected, and is presented in straightforward language as it will affect someone who is no longer working (at least full time), whether he or she is aged 50 or 70.

Each signpost offers practical help and assistance, as well as encouragement which, if followed, should open new vistas and perhaps kindle former interests. Dozens of ideas are explored from folk dancing to hill climbing. But more important is the basic, down to earth approach anyone who has given up work is recommended to adopt to add sparkle and variety to their life.

And if those attributes already exist, there are plenty of tips to give them added vigour!

The book is for reading or browsing, and either method will bring its rewards. Its objective is to show every pensioner how he or she can make so much more of their life. Being retired no longer means being on the scrapheap; on the contrary, it is a unique state which can boast both status and experience, two qualities which younger generations can never claim. For this reason those of more mature years will always have an enviable place in our society, as leaders and mentors of those who follow on behind them.

Used wisely, this book will enrich your life or that of an older person you know.

Preface to Second Edition

Only one thing has changed since the original edition of this book was published and that is the opportunities for those of senior years have become further enhanced!

As the market of retirees grows, so do the suppliers of those goods and services that they demand. It is impossible these days to open a newspaper or magazine without coming across special offers for people over 55 - or, indeed, over 50. Saga will take you on at the earlier age and the Association of Retired Persons even has 'O50' (over 50) as part of its title.

Holidays, car insurance, private health plans, garden plants and implements - all, and more, can be had for a saving if you have reached that magic age.

And magic it is. Providing you have your health and a little cash put aside or a private pension to enjoy yourself, then life is what you are going to make it.

Get out there now and have the time of your life.

Mike Mogano

Solihull; April 1998

1 GETTING YOURSELF UNORGANISED

- You've got it made
- An unnatural state
- Taking charge
- Where to live
- Getting more information

To borrow - and adapt - a phrase, the day you retire will be 'the first day of the rest of a wonderful life'. Given the right approach you can make it much better. And after a lifetime of watching the clock you can even become 'unorganised' - and still make retirement the most exciting period of your life.

You've Got It Made

Today's retirees have it made. Almost all of Britain's ten million pensioners have a significantly higher standard of living and greater disposable income than their predecessors of twenty years ago.

In America pensioners are known as the 'grey panther' brigade because of their power to negotiate lower costs for many popular products and services.

GETTING YOURSELF UNORGANISED

By the year 2030 almost one-third of Britain's population will be pensioners and more than one in ten will be over 75. Average life expectancy is increasing, and by this date will become at birth 78 for men and 83 for women, compared with 73 and 79 years currently. We are getting healthier and living longer.

Pensioner power

Pensioners are now seen as a force to be reckoned with, as opposed to the earlier view of their being a cost to society. They have enormous spending power, a fact the world's major product and service companies are fast beginning to recognise. A recent study of 'third agers' (50 to 75 year olds) by Mintel Research reported that this section of the community owned 80% of Britain's wealth. These people lead an active lifestyle and are not intimidated by fresh ideas or new technology. They account for 30% of all consumer expenditure, spend more on alcohol and gardening, for instance, than any other group and pay out almost £2bn a year on holidays.

In 1997 well over 4,000 centenarians received congratulatory messages from the Queen, compared with the mere 250 recipients in 1953 when the Queen first came to the throne.

So if you have recently retired, or are about to, you will be joining a growing band of people raring to extract more from their lives than ever before. Hopefully, you will also have the physical and financial capabilities to do so and, with careful control, these should both last for as long as you need them.

An Unnatural State

Despite the potential which lies ahead however, retirement is not a natural state for man to find himself in. Homo Sapiens as a race has a tendency to work and in the less developed countries for instance, retirement is unheard of. Only when an older person is unable to wield the plough or the axe any longer will he or she be allowed to 'rest' for the remainder of their life.

In the western world we tend to retire at an age when we are still strong and healthy, yet the primeval pull to work still exists and many people find it extremely difficult to cope with the sudden change from an active working life to one of relative leisure. A small minority regrettably fail to make the change at all and end their lives in a state of suspended disbelief. You, of course, won't be in this category for you have already begun to take advice by reading this book.

Attitude is what counts

Dr. Joyce Brothers, a noted American psychologist, describes retirement as either a time of satisfaction and serenity - or one of resentment, disappointment and fear. She goes on to suggest it all depends on how you emerge from your pivotal decade - the ten years from about forty-five to fifty-five. This is when you begin to sense the arrival of middle age; your attitude towards it will influence the remainder of your life.

Another expert in this field, Professor Alastair Heron, drew up his list of six essential ingredients for a happy, successful retirement. They were:

- An adequate philosophy of life
- An adequate income
- Good health
- Congenial companions
- Purposeful occupation, and
- A congenial home

You will see that, apart from income and health, the remaining ingredients normally fall under your own personal control. Even the two exceptions can be influenced by a determination to remain fit (assuming you start off this way) which in turn may allow you to increase your income, if necessary, through a hobby or interest.

Taking Charge

So you do need to stay in control. Take charge of the situation to keep you, not the system, in the driving seat.

'Life is not a rehearsal' says retirement author Dr. Dorothy Rowe. Now she is a pensioner herself she no longer feels she has to put the world to rights but still enjoys offering her opinion in her specialist field, knowing that the world carries on regardless. This is the attitude we need to adopt.

MAKE THE MOST OF YOUR RETIREMENT

Grey pride

Be proud of your new state and never miss an opportunity to tell others the endless potential it has opened up for you. You now have far more personal choices than ever before. You can decide what time to get up, what time to go to bed, when to take your holidays, when to visit relations. You can throw the clock out of the window at last; no longer are you tied to a demanding work schedule.

But it calls for careful planning. 'You have got to go over a bridge when you retire,' says former football manager Brian Clough. 'You can't just sit in a chair, read papers and watch television. You can't just switch off.'

The danger, of course, is that you can do just that. Without some forethought this is exactly what you might find yourself doing in a month or two's time when the euphoria has faded.

Staying in charge will prevent you from slipping down that slope.

Managing your time

Some people are naturally good managers of their own time; others fail miserably. Only you know in which camp you fall and whether or not you need to put some time aside to improve your habits of a lifetime. It certainly isn't too late to adapt, adopt and improve.

The cry 'I don't have the time' may have been justified - on occasions - during your working life but it won't hold water now. On the assumption that you need an average

GETTING YOURSELF UNORGANISED

amount of sleep, then you have over one hundred and ten hours a week to fill - time enough for a plethora of interests.

Know what you want to do

The first move is to define what objectives you are aiming at - if you know your goals, you are more likely to achieve them. Make a list of what you want to complete in, say, a one month time period. Then split that list down into tasks that will take minutes, those that will take two or three hours and those that might occupy several days. Reduce the total number of tasks immediately by actually completing those that will only take minutes!

Decide when to do it

Now set a timetable allowing for some flexibility and the weather if some of the jobs involve being out of doors. Make a separate list, repeating any tasks that might require a deal of preparation, such as buying paint or taking measurements. Get those preparations out of the way as soon as you can so that there are no hindrances to start dates. You mustn't allow yourself to have any excuses!

You might also like to number your jobs in order of their priorities although those near the bottom must never be neglected; renumber them as you complete the top few so that those lower down become of increasing importance with the passage of time.

MAKE THE MOST OF YOUR RETIREMENT

Be time-thrifty

Never waste journey time. Newspapers and magazines can be read on buses and trains, and language courses played in motor cars. Save non-urgent telephone calls and make them in one fell swoop rather than constantly breaking off from whatever else you are doing. And never get too far behind with your task list.

Managing time is not always easy and interruptions are invariably welcomed, but now that you have more time than ever before treat it like gold dust. Don't let it trickle through your fingers. It's the one commodity you can never replace.

You and your partner

If you are living with someone else, all that we have advised so far is going to take a degree of co-operation. Your partner may still be working but, in any event, must be allowed a view. None of your new-found freedom can be put to very good use unless there is an accord between you. Make sure everyone's cards are on the table before confirming too many new commitments.

Your domestic lifestyle cannot be overlooked. Meals still have to be cooked, groceries bought, shelves dusted and cars cleaned. Perhaps now is a good time to review these menial tasks and consider some different allocation of duties.

Working males rarely get too involved in the cooking process; what about taking this task over two or three days a week? Could taking the dog for a walk be more evenly

GETTING YOURSELF UNORGANISED

shared - or even enjoyed together? When it comes to entertaining, consider sharing the preparation of courses. Is gardening currently the province of only one partner and is this something in which both could now take a renewed interest?

Self-discipline is important and a lack of selfishness imperative. Whilst it would be unwise to take on fresh tasks that become boring chores, it is at least worth experimenting with some new routines for a month or two. They may well prove illuminating - and given time, enjoyable.

Each of you may have established a completely separate pattern of external relationships and, while there is no necessity to disrupt these, some coming together of interests once you are both free of regular work is recommended. Sharing hobbies is by no means compulsory but it does make for more contented domestic arrangements.

. . . or on your own

If you are giving up work and live on your own, then the change can be one of the greatest of all shocks to the system - but one that can be overcome with determination and a little forethought.

Changing from a lifestyle that might have involved seeing and speaking to a large number of people every day to one where contacts must be pre-arranged is a big step in anyone's life. If this mirrors yours and you are feeling a little lonely, do not despair.

Ideally, of course, you will have planned for this transformation during the year or so prior to retirement; but if the change has come as something of a shock to you, a little time and perseverance can overcome it. The chapter on Finding Fresh Interests will provide you with dozens of new ideas, whilst that on Helping in the Community will add some more. There are still, no doubt, family and friends to visit and you can make a start with these; see Chapter 3. And if you feel that a new relationship is not beyond you, take a look at Repartnering in the final chapter.

Getting interested

If you still have difficulty in making regular contact with others, then think about subjects that especially interest you. Start a list and keep it going for a week or two; then tidy it up and prioritise it so that you have perhaps three topics that you enjoy talking about. They may be as basic as 'Going on holiday', 'Knitting' or 'Watching soap operas'; equally they could be as complex as 'International affairs' or 'Motor racing'. It matters not.

Now search the racks of the larger newsagents for journals and magazines dedicated to your topic; buy them regularly. Soon you will be presented with opportunities to write, talk to or meet with others actively interested in your subject. Grab those opportunities. Before you know it, you will have built up a new circle of friends with whom you share a common interest.

If you are on the Internet this will offer you hundreds of opportunities to meet up with (at your choice) others with the same interests. Do check bona fides first though.

GETTING YOURSELF UNORGANISED

Where To Live

This is possibly your most pressing concern, unless you have already taken the decision to stay put. If you have lived in your present house for some years this could indeed be the best 'move'. Uprooting is never easy, and can be even more traumatic if it coincides with a major life-change such as retirement. Many have later regretted moving miles away from a familiar environment at that stage.

There are usually more valid reasons for staying where you are than there are for moving and these could include:

- A social life based around your present neighbourhood.
- Friends and/or family nearby.
- Knowledge of local traders, hospital services, bus routes, etc.
- Awareness of your own property and its demands (or otherwise) for refurbishment, etc as opposed to the unknown problems which might face you in a new property.

Sort out the pros and cons

If you have doubts, take two pieces of paper and write on one the advantages of staying put and on the other the disadvantages. Take your time about this and keep the lists running for a week or two; discuss them with those you can trust. It will soon become clear which list outweighs the other but, if it's a draw, it might be better to remain where you are. However well you research a new home and a new area, there are nearly always unpleasant surprises which come to light soon afterwards.

MAKE THE MOST OF YOUR RETIREMENT

Calculate the cost of moving (not light these days when stamp duty, solicitors' and agents' fees and removal charges are added in) and measure this against the cost of any refurbishment or property changes which would enhance your present home. A smaller bedroom can easily be converted into a study or work room; some people even manage to provide one for each partner!

If you hold leasehold as opposed to freehold property, you may be thinking of purchasing the freehold if it is available. This is not always the preferred option, however, and you should seek both legal and family advice on the matter. Very long leaseholds are as good as freeholds and often involve only minuscule ground rents. You can also get help from the Leasehold Enfranchisement Advisory Service.

There can be, of course, very valid reasons for moving home, such as:

- It really is too large now and is costing too much to run.
- Children and/or grandchildren live too far away to allow you to keep regularly in touch.
- You have not lived in your present house for very long and do not have many local connections.

If these considerations heavily outweigh reasons for staying where you are, then a move may be the wisest course. In this case, take your time in looking around but be very wary of attempting to coincide your retirement

GETTING YOURSELF UNORGANISED

with a house move. It is a significant step you are taking and another six months or so devoted to careful research will pay off in the long run.

Safe and secure

Wherever you decide to live, your own comfort and security become more important in older age, and a few moments standing back and viewing your property with fresh eyes could pay dividends.

On the comfort front there is a wealth of information you can obtain on ensuring your home is warm and draught-free. Loft insulation requirements, for instance, change regularly and you should probably now have at least six inches (150 mm) of suitable material between your joists. Specialists in this field can be tracked down through the National Association of Loft Insulation Contractors. Wall insulation should be investigated if you do not have it installed already; expenditure on this comfort is likely to pay for itself within a few years.

Heat is also lost of course through doors and windows, and double glazing is always worth investigation. The Glass and Glazing Federation will find a local member to do this for you, while the Draught Proofing Advisory Association provides general advice and details of member contractors.

There are other measures you can take to keep warm. Here's an overall checklist:

- Consider wall insulation.
- Check lagging of tanks and insulation in your loft.

MAKE THE MOST OF YOUR RETIREMENT

- Lag hot water pipes where these are vulnerable to colder weather.
- Fit draught-proofing to doors and windows.
- Consider double glazing.
- Does your boiler need an overhaul - or even replacing?
- If your heating system does not have timers and thermostats, add them.
- Use low energy light bulbs.

Accidents in the home account for some forty per cent of this country's total fatal accidents, yet many could easily be avoided. Have your electrical wiring looked over by a competent electrician if it has not been investigated for some years; ensure that there are no rugs or carpets that can be tripped over; have gas appliances checked regularly; and avoid keeping dangerous substances at home. Open fires and portable heaters are best avoided; alternatives are healthier and quite often cheaper to run.

The Association of British Insurers will send you a leaflet on Home Safety if you write to them.

Finally, ask your local Crime Prevention Officer around for a coffee (ring your police station) and seek his advice on burglar alarms, security lights and other measures to keep out unwanted guests. And never open your front door completely to anyone you don't know; fit a chain for safety's sake. A few pounds spent may save lots of trouble later.

GETTING YOURSELF UNORGANISED

Moving abroad

If this is on your agenda you will have major considerations to take into account, and obviously you will need to study the do's and don'ts far into the night before making a move. On your list should be: the careful choosing of a location; acquiring a property, and the finances involved; and how to settle in and acclimatise yourself to a foreign lifestyle.

Never purchase a property abroad when you are on holiday nearby. The sun, sand and perhaps sangria are all likely to over-influence you, and you are better advised to seek out all the details and ponder over them after you return home. For the same reason do not sign any pieces of paper, however harmless they may appear on the surface, nor pay over any money at your holiday site.

A solicitor with a working knowledge of purchasing property in the country you intend to move to is vital. Legal systems abroad are very different from those existing in the UK and you may even find, after paying the full price, that your rights to the property are subservient to someone else's. Foreign states very often interfere in ways that we have not heard of here.

The Financial Times publishes the magazine Resident Abroad which in turn produces a survival kit for anyone contemplating moving abroad. It will help you with tax planning, establishing offshore bank accounts, selecting healthcare and insurance cover and other financial matters of importance to expatriates. If you are retaining property in the UK, it also gives guidance on managing it while you are abroad.

Getting More Information

Seminars and courses

More and more companies, particularly the larger ones, are arranging to send their employees coming up for retirement on a course (usually referred to as a seminar) designed to ease them into that new way of life. If you have the opportunity to attend one, do so and preferably with your partner. They are normally free of charge and many are residential over a weekend or a day or two.

The contents usually revolve around the subjects covered in this book and, where retirement is still a little way off, some time is given to planning ahead. Many are financially based and explain, for instance, what State benefits you may be entitled to, although keeping fit and healthy and finding new leisure activities are other regular items on the programme.

Where such courses are not available to you, you might like to sign up for one with the Pre-Retirement Association of Great Britain and Northern Ireland which runs sessions lasting from one day to a week. Similar courses are run in Scotland by the Scottish Pre-Retirement Council. Other alternatives include courses run by the Workers' Educational Association, the Open University or your local college. Equally there are a number of private concerns offering pre-retirement courses and these may be found in your local Yellow Pages under Educational Services. Check to see whether the course is entirely

GETTING YOURSELF UNORGANISED

independent or whether it is organised by a specific provider of financial services, in which case it may well have a particular bias.

You are likely to find yourself in the company of 20 or 30 like-minded folk, all keen to get as much out of the sessions as possible. Ask your employer if he will sponsor you for the cost.

The Retirement Trust offers a free service for individuals who would like to discuss pre-retirement planning with an expert for an hour or two; this facility is available nation-wide.

The specialists

Retirement is such a big marketplace that it is full of experts ready to offer you their views but be wary, in particular, of those advertising their wares in the field of financial services. Many are quite reputable but others are less so. Perhaps the best rule of thumb is, if you haven't heard of the concern then find another that is well known to you. Seek the advice of your bank manager if you are unsure.

Apart from these, there are several highly respectable organisations which have established themselves in recent years specifically to serve the retired population, or in some cases those over the age of fifty. Make full use of these; membership rates are quite modest and can come with a host of benefits such as free accident insurance and discounts on holidays.

MAKE THE MOST OF YOUR RETIREMENT

Saga and the Association of Retired Persons (known as ARP Over 50) are two of the better known, and both publish regular magazines available on subscription or from major newsagents. ARP Over 50 has well over 130 Friendship Centres up and down the country offering varied programmes of social events as well as 24-hour helplines. Joining either - or both - of these organisations will keep you in touch with special offers and tips which you will almost certainly find beneficial. Saga offers life membership for two at a very reasonable rate.

Other magazines aimed at pensioners include Yours, Choice, Active Life and World of Retirement, all available on the newsagents' shelves.

Although not exclusively for pensioners you may find that the University of the Third Age (U3A) suits your tastes. It is a self-help movement for people no longer in paid work and operates through a national network of regional centres. It runs its own national newspaper published three times a year and many people have found U3A's friendly, down to earth approach to its subjects refreshing.

Now that you have got yourself organised, let's hit the trail to happy retirement . . .

2 RECALCULATING YOUR FINANCES

- Income
- Budgeting
- Taxation
- Seeking advice

There is probably one niggling question uppermost in your mind, and that is 'Will I have sufficient income?'

But sufficient for what? Enough to maintain the lifestyle you have grown accustomed to over several years? Just enough for life's basics: food, shelter and warmth? Or somewhere in-between to provide you, and your partner if you're a twosome, with an adequate level of income for life's necessities - plus a little bit of fun?

Most people will be happy to plump for this last choice and our challenge, therefore, is to create a balance between income and expenditure to make certain it happens.

Income

Income may arise from a variety of sources:

- A pension or annuity from a former employer
- State pension and/or other benefits
- Income from investments
- Capital from, say, a maturing life policy
- Income from a hobby, or from working part-time in retirement

Let's take a closer look at each of these in turn.

Pensions and annuities

If you have not yet retired, you will need to take advice on the different options open to you if you are a member of your company's pension scheme, although where you are eligible to take a lump sum of cash in lieu of part of your pension it is almost always worthwhile to do so; this is known as 'commuting'. This lump sum can then be invested in various ways to provide additional income. If you are self-employed, and have established your own pension scheme, taking advice is still a sensible course. Either way, how you should go about this is covered later in this chapter under Seeking Advice.

You are not obliged to begin taking your pension as soon as you retire especially if you intend to take other work, although the Inland Revenue insists upon your doing so when you reach 75! Generally, if you joined your pension

RECALCULATING YOUR FINANCES

plan before 1 July 1988 then you can start drawing from it on retirement at age 60; if it was after this date then you are entitled to begin drawing at age 50. In either case, if you have had to give up work owing to ill health then you may be allowed to begin earlier. Certain categories of people are allowed by the Revenue to 'retire' earlier still: boxers and models, for instance, at the age of 35! Ask your employer what options are open to you.

Nor do you always have to accept the pension rate offered to you by the company holding your savings. You may be allowed to shop around for a better 'annuity' rate. There are many other factors to consider, though, at this stage, such as:

- Will my pension continue after my death to look after my partner? and
- Is there a guaranteed period during which it will be paid, even if I die beforehand?

These are the sort of questions you should be firing at your personnel manager, pensions manager or independent financial advisor before committing yourself to a particular scheme.

State benefits

Although, of course, many older people have shown that it is possible to exist upon the State pension alone, these are declining in number as more and more retired employees begin to draw benefits from their own personal pension schemes. The State pension, however, to which most people have contributed during their working lifetime, may come as a useful addition when you reach the age of 60 (working women) or 65 (men).

The first thing you should do, in the year or so before retirement, is to complete Form BR19 which you can obtain from the Benefits Agency (Department of Social Security). This will let you know precisely what your pension is going to be, based upon the contributions you have made during your working life. The advantage of doing this is that if you have a shortfall in contributions during the preceding six years, you now have an opportunity of making voluntary payments in order to catch up and thereby improve your final pension. Don't miss out on this vital step.

The State pension may be made up of three parts: basic; State Earnings Related Pension (SERPS); and/or a graduated payment. Generally speaking if you have contributed for between 25% and 90% of what is considered a 'normal' working life (49 years for men; 44 for women), you will be entitled to something, and in the case of having achieved a 'satisfactory' level (90%), you will receive the full pension. Any SERPS addition applies only to employed persons who were not contracted out of this particular scheme. Graduated pensions apply only to the period 1961 to 1975 but don't get too excited about this addition; at most it is likely to be well under £7 per week.

If you are concerned about having paid sufficient basic contributions in periods when you were not working, your forecast, when received, should clarify the situation. To give you a rough guide, in all the following instances,

RECALCULATING YOUR FINANCES

although not working, you will have received credits, equivalent to the basic rate, instead:

- If you were unemployed and had 'signed on' at your local office.
- If you are a man, for the period between the ages of 60 and 65, whether or not you 'signed on'.
- If you have at any time claimed sickness or maternity benefits, or were entitled to invalid care allowance or unemployability supplement.
- If you were taking an approved course of training.
- If you were in full-time education and born after 5 April 1957 in the tax years in which you reached the ages of 16, 17 or 18.

Just as you can defer receiving a personal pension, so are you able to put off the day you start drawing from the State. The benefit of doing this is to increase your ultimate pension by about 7.5% a year for each year you defer. Remember, also, to defer any graduated pension to which you may be entitled, however small, as these are linked to inflation and you would lose out otherwise.

Perhaps the best news on the State front in recent years has been the abolition of the Earnings Rule since 1989. Prior to that date pensioners in their earlier years who earned more than £75 a week saw their State benefit cut. Now there is no limit to the amount you may earn as a pensioner - providing, of course, you remain fit enough to do so!

If you go abroad for more than six months, you can arrange to have your pension (or widow's benefits) paid anywhere you choose. Contact the DSS Overseas Branch.

MAKE THE MOST OF YOUR RETIREMENT

Investment income

Hopefully you will from one source or another have received at least a little capital which you are free to control yourself. It is going to be very important for your future income how you look after this.

We will assume that income is a priority, for it is possible to invest capital aimed almost entirely at future growth (ignoring income) instead. Even so you should consider seeking some growth in at least part of your capital to counter the inevitable effects of inflation; we will look at this again later under Budgeting. At the same time you will naturally be seeking safe shelters for your funds; now is not the time to begin squandering a lifetime's savings.

Safest of all are the Government's various National Savings choices and its issued bonds, still better known as 'gilt-edged' securities (or gilts) as the certificates used to be edged in gold. All of these may be bought through any Post Office, who will let you have the necessary forms, although (at slightly higher cost but you will know precise buying or selling prices) you can also deal in gilts through a stockbroker. If you don't already use one, contact the London Stock Exchange for local availability or use one of the London or provincial brokers by telephone.

The National Savings Pensioners Bond is well worth a look at - and entirely safe - if you are able to tie some of your capital up for five years.

Next, and still relatively safe, are the major banks and building societies who offer between them a plethora of investment schemes as well as, from time to time, special offers for limited periods: watch the newspapers for

RECALCULATING YOUR FINANCES

details. If you want to compare all the available rates, take a year's subscription to 'Money Facts'. One currently attractive method of investment is the 'Escalator' or 'Stepped Income' bond, paying increasing rates of interest over, usually, a 3 to 5 year period.

Keep an eye on the Press, especially the Sunday papers, for details of guaranteed income bonds issued by insurance companies although, if you are not fully familiar with this kind of investment, take advice from a professional first. Some are straightforward and first class; others somewhat complicated and more risky.

The word 'guaranteed' is used somewhat loosely and although it may apply to income levels, this may be at the detriment of your capital.

Finally there is the Stock Market where you can put some of your funds into ordinary shares or Unit or Investment Trusts. These (and especially individual shares) are clearly higher risk than most of the above alternatives but, if you have capital available of, say, more than £50,000 then you should be considering these for a part of your portfolio, once again to offset the ravages of inflation.

Do, however, avoid the specialist markets such as Futures, Options or Commodities unless you are already an expert in these.

Risk can be spread through investing in Unit Trusts which basically hold a 'basket-full' of shares, often in one sector of the market, or in Investment Trusts which are very similar but whose shares (as opposed to units) can be bought and sold on their own account. Remember, however, that any share can fall as well as rise and that price movements - especially short term - are invariably more affected by national and international politics and financial policies than by the underlying performance of the company or companies themselves. Again, seek professional advice.

You should also know about Tax Exempt Special Savings Accounts (TESSAs) which banks, building societies and others offer on a tax-free basis for limited investments over five-year periods. Look also at Personal Equity Plans (PEPs) where any capital gains and interest or dividends are free of tax, although your money is placed in stocks and shares and the warning above still applies. A charge will also be made for running your PEP.

From April 1999, TESSAs and PEPs will be replaced by Individual Savings Accounts (ISAs). The main features of ISAs are as follows:

- Accounts will be guaranteed by the government to run for at least 10 years.
- Up to £5,000 can be saved each year, of which no more than £1,000 can go into cash and £1,000 into life insurance.

RECALCULATING YOUR FINANCES

- For the first year only, £7,000 can be saved of which no more than £3,000 can go into cash and £1,000 into life insurance.
- Accounts will be completely free of tax liabilities.

Do take advice, however, before switching from current PEP or TESSA schemes.

When comparing interest rates of any investment, do not forget (a) that some of these can change from time to time and (b) to calculate what your after-tax return is going to be rather than being impressed by the gross pre-tax rate. Further details appear under Taxation.

Still confused? Remember some basic 'rules':

- Take expert advice unless you are fully familiar with the investment scene.
- Safety should predominate in any retirement portfolio.
- Retain about one year's personal spending in 'liquid', ie readily accessible, funds.
- Spread your money across as reasonably wide a spectrum as it will stretch.

Capital items

You may be lucky enough to receive some additional cash from, say, life policies maturing or from the sale of share options, and similar considerations will apply when you come to invest these. It is almost always unwise, incidentally, to surrender a life policy especially if it has been in existence for some years. Consider instead its sale if you really do need the money now. Telephone the Association of Policy Market Makers for details.

There may still be, though, some existing liabilities around, especially if you have retired earlier than expected. These could include a mortgage on your house, along with any other loans or hire purchase for items such as a car, etc. The big question poses itself - should I pay these off?

As far as a mortgage is concerned, careful forethought is needed. Almost certainly it will pay to reduce it to no more than £30,000 (since there is no tax relief above this figure) and it is probably better to clear it entirely. If you have linked endowment policies consider maintaining these until their normal maturity; earlier surrender could be costly. There may be occasions though, particularly if your income is close to where age-related allowances become due, when you could be worse off through repaying a mortgage, so do take advice.

With other loans and hire purchase, the borrowing rate is nearly always bound to be higher than investment rates so it makes sense to repay these.

What else could you do with any 'surplus' cash? If you have been used to a company-run car, replacing this will take a little, depending upon taste! Gifts to the family will always be welcomed, particularly at levels which do not attract subsequent inheritance tax - see where I discuss this later. If there is sufficient cash, you may be considering a holiday home but do discuss this with family and friends in some detail before committing yourself. White elephants are not for purchasing at this critical time of your life!

Finally, what about splashing out and going on that world cruise? Why not indeed, providing it leaves sufficient in the kitty to give you the level of income you are seeking.

Earned income

If you feel the need, or desire, to carry on working, even part-time, then firstly take stock of your abilities, knowledge and experience to avoid selecting the wrong job. Some retraining may be desirable, especially if you want to make a complete break.

Don't rush into anything, and before you make a choice, familiarise yourself with your local Jobcentre, employment agencies and newspaper and radio advertising of jobs available locally. Take advice on completing a basic curriculum vitae (CV) which should then be tailored to particular vacancies. Narrow it down if necessary to no more than two A4 pages and ensure that it emphasises your strengths.

Your home can provide additional income, either in the form of taking in lodgers or running a 'bed and breakfast' service. Annual rental income of less than £3,250 a year does not have to be declared to the Inland Revenue, providing it is your only or main home, under the Government's 'Rent-a-Room' scheme.

Home income plans, under which you mortgage a part of your house in return for immediate income, are only for those over 69 (in the case of couples a combined age of over 145) and specialist independent advice is essential first. A national body, Safe Home Income Plan (SHIP) has been formed to help restore confidence in these schemes.

MAKE THE MOST OF YOUR RETIREMENT

SHIP guarantees that its customers may live in their properties for life or move if they wish. Risky investments have been outlawed. Look for SHIP's logo.

Also worth considering, if you find the need to raise money, is the Bank of Scotland's Shared Appreciation Mortgage (SAM). Version one allows you to borrow cash against your home in return for sharing a percentage of any future increases in value; no interest is payable. Upon redemption any increase in value is split on a pre-agreed basis between you (or your heirs) and the Bank. The second version involves paying interest but, to compensate for this, you take a larger proportion of any value increase when the mortgage is repaid. Minimum property valuations are £60,000 and the minimum loan is £15,000. You can opt out of the scheme at any time so are not locked in for 'life'.

A book entitled 'Using Your Home as Capital' is published by Age Concern at £4.95

Some retirees do successfully turn their hobbies into cash cows; but do study the marketplace in some depth and remember that you are unlikely to be fully remunerated for your time. If it's something you enjoy and it can earn you pin-money, that's another matter.

Remember the impact that any additional earnings will have on your tax bill and the fact that you may be liable for National Insurance payments; seek an accountant's advice before proceeding. If you are going to set up in business on your own (or with a partner) then there are a myriad of legal and financial aspects to think about: see

RECALCULATING YOUR FINANCES

'How to Start and Run Your Own Business' by this author published by Graham and Trotman Limited (now Kluwer Law International) of London.

Budgeting

There are likely to be some major changes in your spending habits following retirement and, for peace of mind, it is essential that you take paper and pencil (you'll be doing some rubbing out!) and draw up your personal budget - even if you have never done so before. It is really quite easy.

Whilst inflation is inevitable, don't try to make allowance for it at this stage; work in today's pounds only. Later you can attempt a few adjustments, bearing in mind that since 1982 inflation has averaged 5% each year. In practical terms this means that today's £1,000 could be worth only £780 in five years' time; if you have an inflation-proofed pension this is less of a worry, if not then you must either find another £220 from somewhere or cut your cloth accordingly.

The income side of your budget should be fairly easy although use the after-tax figure; see Taxation below.

Expenditure

Expenditure will require a few headings which should encompass all your costs. Try Home, Garden, Maintenance, Transport, Pets, Holidays, Gifts, Sports and

Hobbies, Insurances, Health, Clothing, Mortgage/Loans/ Hire Purchase, Entertaining, Subscriptions, Church: this should take care of most of them.

Treat everything on a monthly basis. Even if you feel you need, say, £4,000 every three years to replace your car, put this in at £111 per month (£4,000 divided by 36). You won't, of course, need that money every month but it will have to be saved unless you have the bonus of a capital injection. Only by adopting this method will you be certain that you are not going to be living beyond your net income.

You should find it possible to make some savings. National Insurance and pension payments will cease, as may lunch costs, travelling to and from work and finding extra money for working clothes. And then look out for discounts for pensioners, free passes and 0% finance. Saving pennies will save you pounds in the long run.

There could be a few additional costs. If you're spending more time at home, then lighting and heating bills may rise. Items like hobbies or sports could demand more of your wallet and you may also find yourself taking more holidays.

If monthly costs look like being less than net monthly income, you'll sleep at night. But if things are the other way round, now is the time to take action. Either you will have to improve your income or find ways of curtailing expenditure. Neither of these courses is likely to be easy, but do discuss them with friends or relations who may provide solutions. What you cannot afford to do is to bury your head in the sand.

RECALCULATING YOUR FINANCES

State help

The State may help. Income support is available for low earners to cover part of the cost of basics such as food, rent or clothing, or even to assist with buying, say, a washing machine. Visit your DSS office or Citizens Advice Bureau.

Taxation

It is not as difficult as you might imagine to calculate your own tax bill and now that you have retired, you will have a little more time to do so! There are plenty of quite readable pamphlets available through tax offices, and bodies such as the Consumers' Association provide useful templates to guide you. The tax year runs from 6th to 5th April and everyone is independently assessed.

Self assessment

Depending upon the complexity of your income you may now have to complete a Self Assessment form. These are somewhat daunting at first but can be got used to! Alternatively, an accountant will complete it for you (at a cost), or computer software is available relatively inexpensively.

MAKE THE MOST OF YOUR RETIREMENT

You can work it out - roughly

To obtain a rough idea of your tax bill, simply deduct your own allowances from that part of your income which is taxable and see how much you are liable to pay at the varying rates. Here's an example for a married couple:

Total Income	£ 25,000
Less any tax-free income (eg National Savings) Less allowances Personal £4,195 Married* £1,900 Total £6,095	- £ 500 - £ 6,095
Taxable Income	**£ 18,405**
First £4,300 @ 20%= £860 Next £14,105 @ 23%= £3,244 Total £4,104 Total after tax Plus untaxed income + (from savings and allowances above)	- £ 4,104 £ 14,301 +£ 6,595
Net Income * aged under 65	**£ 20,896**

This is a simplified example; there is a 40% rate which comes in at taxable income of £26,100 and full relief is not now given on the Married Allowance but this gives you an idea of how simple the calculation can be. If you or your partner is over 65 you may also be able to claim age-related allowances.

RECALCULATING YOUR FINANCES

Take advantage of any breaks

Since you are taxed independently, it may be wise to split any investments between you to keep tax bills to a minimum. Each of you can realise £6,800 of capital gains in each tax year without incurring any additional liability. There is no tax to pay on PEP or TESSA income, nor on gains on Government securities unless your holding is exceptionally high. There are also forms available at banks and building societies which will allow you to receive gross interest if you are not liable for tax.

Some other reliefs against tax can be claimed such as payments on the first £30,000 of a mortgage on your only or main home, but only at a 10% tax rate. If you covenant charitable gifts or make payments under the Gift Aid Scheme you can also avoid paying tax on these. Tax relief is no longer claimable on the costs of private medical subscriptions.

Check out overseas residence

If you have elected to live abroad, the tax position may well be very different and you should seek advice from the Overseas Branch of the DSS.

Inheritance tax

Your family will eventually benefit if you begin even now considering the alternatives to paying what is known as an 'optional' tax.

In the case of a married couple after the second death, inheritance tax (currently at 40%) is payable on an estate worth in excess of £223,000; this includes the net value (after mortgages) of your property and all other non-trust assets including the proceeds of life policies. It is thus not very difficult to accumulate this sum, and in the case of an estate of, say, £250,000, the tax man will come knocking for £11,000. Yet this can easily be avoided.

Reduce the future tax bill now

Wills are covered more fully in Chapter 10 but if you haven't already made a will, do so now. Take professional advice (from your bank or a solicitor) and discuss the ways in which you might eliminate, or at least reduce, your eventual tax bill. These will include making regular gifts of capital and putting some assets into discretionary trusts, although there are both benefits and snags to the latter. Equally, you can invest in a life policy which will remain outside your estate (and that of your partner's) and be available to your beneficiaries to meet some, or all, of any inheritance tax due.

To add to the complications, there is a possibility that the Government will make changes to this tax, and this emphasises the need to take professional advice. Any costs will be more than saved when it comes to your nearest and dearest paying out your inheritance tax liability. So take action now!

Seeking Advice

As far as your own pension is concerned, if you work for a large company someone will normally be able to help with your queries; make an appointment and go armed with your questions. If this proves less helpful than you had hoped, try the Occupational Pensions Advisory Service; they offer guidance to any member of an occupational scheme.

When it comes to investing your hard-earned funds, this is another matter. Unless you are an expert you will need an independent financial advisor and one way of finding half a dozen in your area is to ring Independent Financial Advisors. Alternatively, get in touch with the Financial Intermediaries, Managers and Brokers' Regulatory Association (FIMBRA) or the Life Assurance and Unit Trust Regulatory Organisation (LAUTRO). The former regulates independent financial advisors and the latter those companies which provide life assurance, unit trusts and pension services. The Personal Investment Authority may in time take over these powers.

Look before you leap

If you know a friendly accountant, then seek him out also, but be aware that he may be a specialist in a particular field or an agent of one company and not therefore entirely suitable to guide you. Banks provide similar advice; some of them are independent but others sell only their own products. Ask at the outset.

MAKE THE MOST OF YOUR RETIREMENT

Finally, a few basic essentials:

- Don't jump into the first investment that you find attractive. Spend a month or two scanning the market-place and in the interim put your capital in a readily accessible, high interest bank or building society account.

- Talk to as many experts as you can find; their advice may sometimes conflict but there should be a common thread running throughout.

- Clarify in your own mind approximately what you are seeking before you talk to others; this will allow you to ask the right questions.

- Be prepared to answer a lot of questions; a good adviser will want to know a lot about you before he makes specific suggestions.

- Always ask whether or not an adviser is entirely independent.

- Don't pay anybody up-front and check bona fides before making out cheques.

If you stick to these 'rules', your money should find relatively safe havens and you will be able to sleep at night. Pleasant dreams!

3 FAMILY AND FRIENDS

- The two of you
- Enjoying grandchildren
- Acting as carer
- Friends
- Keeping in touch

Age teaches us one important thing - to appreciate more the people around us and less the material possessions that we once saw as having overriding priority. As we advance through life we prefer to find more time for family and friends, and it is then that we really begin to understand the true importance of friendship. If you have still to retire, this may not have hit you yet - but it will.

Everyone's situation will, naturally, be different and you might have very little 'family', or you may be part of a big crowd. You may relish a hectic social life, or you might prefer to do most things on your own or with just a partner. Everyone welcomes occasional periods of being completely alone, even the big party-givers. But don't cut yourself off entirely from other people; contact (if only from time to time) is going to be increasingly important to you now you have a different lifestyle. And if you don't currently have many contacts, give serious thought to widening that circle, if only by a little.

The Two Of You

Let's assume there are two of you and let's call your coupling 'marriage' whether or not this is the case. Things are going to change, that's the message.

A period of adjustment

Possibly, being in each other's company for up to twelve or more hours each and every day is a very different outlook from the one you have been used to. It will call for some adjustments. Not only from yourself but from your partner too.

You may consider you already have a perfect marriage and are looking forward to spending more time in each other's company. That is a superb, positive start. For many people, however, the prospect can be a daunting one, especially if one partner is still out at work for most of each weekday. Will she - or he - expect the other to have a meal ready at the end of the day? Will one be tired while the other has rested and is raring to go? How will these two apparently incompatible situations reconcile themselves?

Talk about it

The answer lies in communication. Each partner has to be open and honest with the other, and not be afraid of expressing their fears. Once views have been put on the table they can be analysed, investigated and resolved. A

FAMILY AND FRIENDS

full resolution is not always necessary as long as each of you has had the opportunity of airing your feelings. Time will cure most differences, providing you can keep animosity out of it.

Some reprogramming may be called for. Almost inevitably some aspects of your lifestyle, and perhaps those of your partner, will change. But discuss them freely beforehand and they will be changes for the better. Honesty is the only policy for this situation.

Enjoying Grandchildren

The chances are that you are already doing just this, for the average age at which parents become grandparents in the UK is forty-seven. Now, however, you have some real time in which to add to that enjoyment.

If you are still waiting, the prospect may admittedly be a daunting one. To think of yourself as a grandfather or grandmother initially comes as a shock; rest assured that, once it becomes a reality, you will be over the moon. It will not be too long before you are boring friends and family with the fact!

You might have to wait until grandchildren grow up a little, though. Babies can seem boring to some people. But wait until that first smile, or those first tentative steps, or indeed when they start calling you 'Grandpa' or 'Grandma'. Then you will experience joys not previously known.

MAKE THE MOST OF YOUR RETIREMENT

You can play a role

Hopefully, you will have more time to spend with your grandchildren in their formative years. Indeed, your choice of home upon retirement may have been influenced by this, as discussed in an earlier chapter. You may have the opportunity of relieving their parents of the burden of looking after them from time to time, and your role as 'surrogate parent' on these occasions can be a vital one to their proper development. Grandparents are always looked up to by children, and whatever you tell - and teach - them, they will believe. Don't miss out on these golden opportunities to shape the next-but-one generation.

Your rights

Sadly, some grandparents see very little of their grandchildren. And there are occasions when, perhaps due to divorce or separation, they are disbarred from doing so. Since the introduction of the Children Act in 1991, grandparents can now seek a court order giving them permission to see the children, or even have them live with them in exceptional circumstances. If the child concerned is old enough, the courts will seek their views. See your solicitor in these cases or write to Children Need Grandparents. The National Council for One Parent Families has a booklet on the topic.

FAMILY AND FRIENDS

Acting As Carer

One irony of people living longer is that carers, particularly of aged parents, frequently retire themselves with their carer role still continuing. Lots of help is available though, and you must not give in to despair if you fall into this category. For one thing you will certainly not be alone.

For the older person involved, little will have changed. But you may now feel more restricted in your movements simply because you have more free time available. As long as you recognise this danger signal, and prepare for it, you should be able to overcome this new feeling of frustration.

Time for a move?

If the aged parent is still at home with you, is now the time to consider alternative accommodation in a nearby nursing or geriatric home? Try to dispense with any feelings of guilt (quite natural in the circumstances). Rational alternatives must always be considered and may, at the end of the day, be better for everyone concerned. Discuss these with as many people as possible, including medical advisers, to help you reach what is always going to be a difficult decision.

Time to adapt?

In cases of more able parents your financial position (capital as opposed to income) may have improved to the extent of being able to adapt your home or that of your parents. Your local authority may help with the cost, and enquiries should be made either through the relevant GP or the Social Services Department. Care and Repair Ltd is the umbrella headquarters for projects aimed at helping older people adapt their own homes. Renovation or minor works assistance grants may be available; speak to your local council.

The Royal Association for Disability and Rehabilitation is a national body specialising in this field. Elsewhere contact the Wales Council for the Disabled, Disability Scotland or Disability Action (Northern Ireland).

Consider the need for alarm systems, including a personalised device from which a message can be sent 24 hours a day. This is available through Aid-Call, and could be useful if you are going to be away more frequently now.

The Benefits Agency produces a very helpful brochure (FB 31) outlining the kinds of help available where you are caring for someone else. A useful guide to the financial, emotional and practical aspects of caring is 'Make the Most of Being a Carer' by Ann Whitfield, also in the Need2Know series. See the back of this book for more details.

Friends

It may not be necessary for you to make new friends; your social cup may already be bubbling over. If so skip this section, but remember all those extra hours you're going to have to fill!

FAMILY AND FRIENDS

New interests, new friends

The easiest way of adding to your acquaintances (and subsequently your friends) is through your leisure interests, so a close look at Chapter 6 may be advisable. As soon as you introduce yourself to a new pastime it will throw up a fresh circle of people with a common interest from whom you can select your new friends.

There's no magic to it. That's how people make friends. They go along to discuss something that interests them, and before they know it, they are in conversation with former complete strangers, all chatting about the same subject. Age is no barrier when a common interest exists.

If you do want to stick to people of a similar age, however, consider joining one of the 120 Friendship Centres operated by the powerful Association of Retired Persons which now caters for anyone over 50. Members follow national issues and also have the option of meeting socially at convenient centres. A well-produced quarterly magazine comes with the subscription price.

The National Pensioners Convention has one and a half million members and also runs social programmes across the country.

Old friends

Now that you have the time, you may care to make contact with friends of bygone years such as armed service companions. These may be contacted through the Royal British Legion.

MAKE THE MOST OF YOUR RETIREMENT

Regimental and other reunions are held from time to time, often abroad, and these visits can form the core of some wonderful companionship. Whether you served in the World War or in one of the later conflicts involving Britain, you will find an organisation dedicated to keeping compatriots together.

Try also CANUSPA (Canada, Australia, New Zealand, USA and Associates) or the Lions Club locally.

Channel 4 Teletext (page 681) has a service called Lost Touch through which you can trace long-lost friends and relations. You will also be surprised to see what reaction you might obtain from placing an advertisement in the national press but check bona fides first before agreeing to meet people.

Church communities

If the church is already part of your life, there is even better reason to continue this into retirement now that you have more time to devote to it.

But if you are beginning to regret your lack of faith, now is an opportunity to reconsider your attitude and make contact with your local church community. No-one is going to ask you where you have been for the last thirty or forty years; generally you will be met with welcome arms and a loving spirit.

If you have a choice of churches and are not committed to a particular faith, visit more than one and make comparisons. Churches do vary - just like shops, pubs and other organisations - and you are likely to feel a more

FAMILY AND FRIENDS

kindred spirit in one than in another. Have no qualms about this; they mostly represent the Christian ethic and differ only in minor views and attitudes.

Find one in which you feel comfortable with the service, the vicar and the people. Before you know it, you will be part of that community and it could even change the rest of your life for the better.

If there is a branch of Toc H in your area, go along to see what they are about. Toc H follows no particular faith, but has a Christian basis and helps people to live open-handedly with their neighbours. There are lots of opportunities for involvement if you so wish, including conservation work, friendship groups and community service projects.

Penfriends

Another way of finding new friends is to use one of the penfriend agencies which have become popular in recent years.

They are ideal for testing out relationships, by letter and/or telephone, before arranging a meeting should you wish to do so. This kind of contact is ideal for those less able to get out and about, and it has helped thousands to combat loneliness. Lifelong friendships can start with a letter to a stranger and, if you enjoy writing, you should give this a try.

Penpals can be found through membership of Saga, while two organisations which help lonely women keep in touch with each other are Solitaire and the National Association of Widows Penclub. Friends by Post caters for both sexes and they run a free service.

Special friends

If you are alone, and wish to meet that 'special someone', you can help that happen - although it is no easier in older age than when you were eighteen! See the section in Chapter 10: Repartnering.

Keeping In Touch

You may be in the lucky position of having a great number of friends and relatives who welcome overnight visits from you, in which case your golden opportunity has arrived now you are retired. But don't push your luck. An annual or bi-annual visit, in some cases, may be delightful for both parties, but if you suggest you call again in a month's time, things might turn a little sour. Most people enjoy having visitors to stay - always by pre-arrangement - but the welcome can be outstayed.

Plan visits

Draw up a list of people who might welcome shorter visits from you; this might include friends or relations whom you have not seen for years simply because there was never enough time. Now decide upon frequencies; it might be weekly for grandchildren (depending upon distances

FAMILY AND FRIENDS

involved), or quarterly for good, but not particularly close, friends. Then tie these into a calendar with suggested dates and, finally, ensure these are entirely convenient to the other parties.

Listen carefully

Mutually-agreed dates are essential. You must listen carefully to the other's views, in case, without actually saying so, they are suggesting that a visit when they might be on holiday (but at home) is not convenient. They may have their own plans, which could include refurbishing part of the house, and when your presence could be a hindrance!

However, if it is clear that your visit is to include baby-sitting duties, this may make a different story entirely! Whatever the circumstances, make certain they suit both parties to a 't' before putting them in place.

Cheap travel

Look at some of British Rail's special offers for pensioners, and for off-peak travel, before firming up on how you are going to get to your destination. Senior Railcards are issued to anyone over the age of 60, entitling you to a third off most normal fares, as well as many other concessions. In the south-east, Network Cards offer a third off most standard fares after 10am on weekdays and at weekends and Bank Holidays. If you're going as far as mainland Europe, look at what Rail Europe Senior Cards can do for you.

MAKE THE MOST OF YOUR RETIREMENT

Most bus and coach firms also offer discounts, such as the third off which National Express apply to senior citizens. And if you're travelling by air, enquire before booking to see whether discounts apply.

Return visits

Expect to return hospitality for frequently visited friends or relations, although one or two nights at weekends is the norm here. Real friends don't expect the Ritz treatment but try and plan beforehand what you feel they would like to do and see, to make their stay more memorable.

On the telephone

One item of expenditure likely to rise in retirement is your telephone bill, although with increasing competition in the UK services are getting progressively better for consumers. BT has recently announced local calls for 1p a minute at weekends, so - providing you're careful - you shouldn't run up too big a bill.

Special schemes are now available for frequently called numbers - such as the Friends and Family, Best Friend and Premier Line arrangements - so make sure you know about these. If you have relatives abroad and want to incorporate three parties in your calls, try the Three Way Calling option for a small quarterly charge.

And if you're worried about other people using your telephone (if you have lodgers, for instance) the Call Barring service is available, also from BT.

FAMILY AND FRIENDS

Through the post

We have already touched on pen-friend services but hopefully you will now find more time to write to old friends and family at a distance. If you have never been much of a letter writer give it a fresh chance. It's so much easier to put your real thoughts and feelings into a letter when other distractions are not present.

Try writing on some of the very attractive cards or notelets available quite cheaply in the shops today; most people love receiving these. And if all your letters do not receive a reply, don't worry; they will still have been well received and appreciated.

Letters do not have to be long, nor confined to special occasions such as birthdays or Christmas. An unexpected letter is the best kind.

At Christmas try adopting the American habit of sending a 'round robin' letter to friends and relations infrequently seen, outlining your own year and its highlights. An up-to-date photograph will bring it to life. And don't forget the personalised Christmas card to go with it!

Living abroad

This will change your circumstances considerably, as we discussed in the first chapter, but keeping in touch with family and friends will of course be more difficult. You will have recognised and considered this when you made your decision to move.

MAKE THE MOST OF YOUR RETIREMENT

Writing letters home will be your cheapest form of contact, while using the telephone fairly frequently will run up a large bill. An alternative is to make your own audio cassettes, or even video cassettes if systems are compatible. These can be quite exciting when received but, in the case of videos, keep them short (say 10 to 15 minutes) if you don't want to bore the folks back home. For an added interest, why not attend video-making courses at your local college?

To keep abreast of events in Britain listen to the BBC World Service, although with the advances in satellite television you should be able to pick up English-speaking programmes in most parts of the world. And your previously local newspaper, or county magazine, will probably despatch copies to you for a small postal premium.

FAMILY AND FRIENDS

Going into hospital

Should this occur, you will want family and friends to rally round, even if it is only to look after the dog or cat as opposed to visiting you!

If you expect to go into hospital, rather than it being merely a possibility, you will, I hope, have taken this into account when deciding upon your retirement base. But if you are at some distance, through choice or accident, try not to be too demanding when it comes to visiting time. Working families find it difficult enough to fit in all their duties without a call for hospital visits.

If it looks like running into a long stay, remember that your State pension will be reduced after six weeks with the NHS.

4 LOOKING AFTER YOUR HEALTH

- Practise preventive healthcare
- Exercise
- Watch for wear and tear...
- Some possible problems

Have you considered what retirement really means in terms of longevity? On the assumption that you are now around the age of 60 and in reasonable health, you have ahead of you - on average - nearly twenty more years to make the most of, without the responsibility of that daily work schedule. What's important though, is to enjoy it, and the only way you can ensure that is to stay healthy. That clearly establishes your number one priority.

Practise Preventive Healthcare

Surprisingly perhaps, this is far simpler than you might imagine. Apart from taking care with what you eat and drink (which we discuss in Chapter 5), a few simple rules will maintain a current healthy state. Certain parts of your body will be more susceptible to wear and tear than others and it is upon those that we must concentrate our efforts:

LOOKING AFTER YOUR HEALTH

they all appear in detail in this chapter. The first thing to establish is your current state of health - not fitness; that is something different.

Have a check-up

You may have already had a thorough appraisal of your body, perhaps with a company scheme or through your own efforts. If so, well done. But if it is some time since your last thorough check (more than two years, say) now is the time to invest a few hundred pounds in yourself and arrange another. It will be money well spent and will provide you with the springboard you need to make any adjustments to ensure you really are going to enjoy that twenty years or more ahead of you. You may be deterred from having this check-up by others yet to be convinced. Ignore them, for they probably have something to hide and are afraid to attend themselves.

Preventive medicine is becoming much more fashionable and is evident, for instance, within the dentistry profession. Before too long, regular overall body checks will be commonplace. We already see this in the Government's breast screening and smear-test programmes. It is a fact of life that older people are more likely to have unsuspected difficulties which, caught at an early stage, can be put right without fuss or concern. Over 20% of tests on 55-plus year olds reveal such problems. So don't delay.

Health checks are entirely confidential and take place in relaxed, pleasant surroundings. Allow a couple of hours, although you may need to spend a further half-hour or so completing a comprehensive form beforehand. Talk to your GP to see what is available on the NHS or telephone BUPA or BMI which, between them, have approaching 50 screening centres in the country. Nuffield Hospitals also provide health screening and there are discounts for Saga members.

Your General Practitioner

Nine out of ten of you will be entirely satisfied with your present doctor, but surveys suggest that a small proportion of the population remains dissatisfied. If you fall into this category it may not have seemed too important until now but, with advancing years, you are advised to shop around in order to strike up a good relationship with someone who could become vital to your continuing health.

You can change your doctor

It is quite easy to change your doctor although you do have to find one that will accept you. Don't forget, out of courtesy, to tell your old practice that you are leaving. They may or may not ask you why, but don't be afraid of explaining your reasons if you feel they are genuine. If you are not certain what alternatives are available in your locality, look in your telephone directory for your Family Health Services Authority (in Scotland your Health Board) who will have a complete list. They will also have a brochure entitled 'You and Your GP'.

LOOKING AFTER YOUR HEALTH

Private GP consultations, as opposed to those provided by the NHS, are considered later. But you may find it more difficult outside of London to find a GP who will take you on as a private patient - although it is possible to use one from time to time and still remain on a GP's NHS register.

Financial help

Remember that if you are over 60 your prescriptions now come free, and this will also apply if you are younger but your income is very low. Department of Health form P11 incorporates a claim form.

Attendance allowance is payable to anyone aged over 65 needing help with personal care because of an illness or disability. You do not normally need a medical examination to qualify and the allowance comes free of tax and independent of your savings. Contact your local Benefits Agency.

Private medical insurance

About ten per cent of the population already have private health insurance, and the number is growing rapidly - although it is useful to remember exactly what the premiums buy you. The quality of advice, and subsequent treatment you receive, will be no different than under the NHS, although you will have a choice as to which specialist you use. Your premiums will buy you time and, whilst the fairness of this is sometimes questioned, the fact remains that private insurance also buys you convenience. Within reasonable parameters you will be able to choose when you go into hospital and avoid, therefore, family anniversaries, reunions, holiday periods and the like.

Company schemes

If you have been lucky enough to be included in a company scheme while you were working, find out if your insurer will keep you on favourable terms following your retirement. Some schemes, although they are becoming fewer, continue to include company pensioners at no cost.

Shop around

If you do have to shop around, make a number of comparisons before you come to a final decision. Terms and conditions vary considerably. Some have particular exclusions and most enforce capping limits which, in more serious cases, could mean your having to top up costs yourself. In London, because hospitals there charge more, the premiums are higher than elsewhere.

Budget policies can be attractive and are well worth looking at, especially if you are prepared to pay an excess premium (just like motor insurance) yourself. Hospital cash plans are also available which provide a pre-agreed sum for every night you are hospitalised; the British Health Care Association has a list of these.

LOOKING AFTER YOUR HEALTH

PPP Healthcare run a scheme called Lifetime Care to meet the costs of care in your own home or a nursing home should an accident or illness befall you.

Alternative treatments

There is not space here to discuss the multitude of alternative therapies and medicines on the market today. An ever-increasing number, however, are becoming available on the NHS after years in the wilderness. In particular many - like chiropractic for instance- are now recommended to complement conventional medicine. And thousands swear by other alternative remedies such as acupuncture, homeopathy, and so forth.

Check carefully first

Many complementary treatments remain controversial, however, and you will have to make up your own mind, after consultations with others, before proceeding. Beware that some treatments which appear on the surface harmless can have side-effects on some people. A visit to a natural health shop will show you what's on offer, and they will usually have a range of books covering other remedies.

Arthritis Care, as an example, has produced a useful booklet (suggested donation £1.50 plus an A4 s.a.e.) called 'The Balanced Approach'.

Exercise

You will almost certainly have heard by now that you must continue exercising, albeit gently, into retirement. The converse, of course, is that if you haven't yet started, now is the time to do so!

Older people lose their strength at the rate of about 2 per cent each year, and exercise is the process which increases muscle tone and therefore keeps aches and pains to a minimum. If it's new to you, you must start gradually. 'Exercise for Healthy Ageing' is a useful booklet available for a suggested donation of £3 from Research into Ageing.

Fit body, fit mind

Being fit means four things:

- Having sufficient strength to lift the shopping and pick up smaller grandchildren!
- Having enough stamina to get through the day without constant lapses of breath.
- Being sufficiently mentally alert to add up a column of figures, say, or convert kilograms to pounds.
- Having a body supple enough to allow you to climb stairs fairly easily, and bend and stretch at will.

LOOKING AFTER YOUR HEALTH

If you keep yourself active, both physically and mentally, you will not have any trouble with the above. You won't expect, of course, to achieve what you could in your thirties, or even forties, but don't let anyone tell you that growing older means you slow down dramatically. Just look at all those 60 and 70-year-olds on the golf course!

Exercise you enjoy

What kind of exercise you undertake is best left to you. Cycling and swimming are two of the best all-round activities you could undertake; but if you've never been on a bike in your life, now is probably not the time to start. Nor do many 60-year-olds find it easy to learn to swim. So decide upon something that is going to suit you. It must be convenient, reasonably moderate, fit your budget and, most important of all, be enjoyable.

If you're a keen gardener, then certainly activities like digging, hoeing and raking will qualify - but don't overdo it. Brisk walking improves stamina but does little for suppleness or strength. Golf is really little more than a country walk punctuated by periods of frustration, but tennis and badminton are another matter and entirely suitable. Squash, unless you are already a regular, is not advised. Dancing, especially the disco variety, will help stamina and suppleness, as will yoga. Bowling will certainly help, and even moderate housework adds to your score. Whatever you choose, remember that it needs to be done fifty-two weeks in the year and outdoor activities may have to alternate with indoor ones.

Don't overdo it

What you should avoid is anything which is clearly over-exerting your body. Nature is a wonderful self-checker, and your heart or your lungs, or perhaps your limbs, will soon let you know if you are asking too much of them. Never hold your breath and make a great effort at doing something like pushing a car or lifting a particularly heavy weight.

It is generally accepted that three or four sessions a week, each lasting a minimum of twenty minutes, is about the right level of aerobic exercise for most people. The super-fit will, of course, manage more! During these periods the heart should be pumping at above normal rate but you should not be abnormally out of breath. If you are new to exercise, then obviously you must work towards this ideal and take things steadily at first.

Your local college will probably run keep-fit courses for older people, sometimes segregating men and women if you prefer this.

Overweight is just as likely to be due to lack of sufficient exercise as to poor eating habits, according to researchers at the Medical Research Council. A recent national survey accused us as a nation of burning off fewer calories than our forefathers, partly because we watch far more television, so be warned!

Watch For Wear And Tear . . .

Your joints

Whatever forms of exercise (variety will help) you select, consider the effect they will have upon your arms, legs and neck. (We look at your back in the next section.) Your joints will certainly benefit from regular usage and if you can maintain this when exercising, you will be killing two birds with one stone. Sports such as tennis and badminton, therefore, will do the job for you, as will dancing, but cycling, for instance, won't do a lot for your arms - just look at all those skinny Tour de France riders!

Daily dozen

Over six million people in this country suffer from arthritic or rheumatic pains and you should vow now not to join their number if at all possible. Start each day with some limbering up activities that can even be done in bed!

- Lay fully on your back with your legs together and horizontal and your arms by your sides. Now bend your knees fully, pulling them into your stomach, if necessary with your arms. Then straighten them again. You can stretch your legs together or one at a time as you prefer.
- Next lift your arms (together or singly again), stretch them as far back as they will go and return them to the lying position.
- Finally bend your elbows, wrists and ankles one at a time.

Do each of these exercises twelve times and you will be doing a great deal towards keeping arthritis at bay. Arthritis Care will provide you with help and guidance if necessary.

Your back

This is worth a section of its own simply because four out of five of us suffer from back pain at some stage in our lives. Sometimes this pain is related to disease of the spine but in most cases it is due to lack of proper care.

Man was originally designed to get along on all fours, and if we now find it more convenient to use only two of those we must pay the consequences. We ask a lot of our spine each day, in addition to merely supporting the weight of our head. We bend it this way and that, and quite often expect it to support us when we attempt to lift something a little beyond our normal capabilities. And then we 'thank' it by bending it up in a chair or laying it on a far from firm mattress. Is it any wonder that it begins to complain?

To keep it happy, try three simple rules:

- Never, never over-exert yourself when lifting heavy items: obtain help.
- Maintain an upright posture at all times - and that includes when walking, and sitting in either armchairs or dining chairs.
- Use a reasonably firm mattress and no more than one pillow at night.

LOOKING AFTER YOUR HEALTH

If you are troubled, try the National Back Pain Association for help.

Your heart

You probably already know that heart diseases are the UK's biggest killer and that risk is increased if:

- you are overweight
- you smoke
- you have high blood pressure
- you are subject to a lot of stress
- you rarely exercise

or

- there is a history of heart disease in your direct family.

Let's see how easy it is to avoid all but the last of these. If you have been exercising regularly, then you probably won't be overweight. If you are retired, stress should normally be minimal and high blood pressure probably absent. If you smoke, stop. There - you've increased your chances of living by a major leap. There really is no excuse.

What you eat and drink is considered in Chapter 5. The rest is up to you. Don't deny yourself the chance of living a lot longer. Send for a free 'Making the Most of Retirement' pack from the British Heart Foundation.

MAKE THE MOST OF YOUR RETIREMENT

Hearing

If you are over 60 and can still hear as well as you could when you were a lot younger, you are in a lucky minority. The wear and tear process reduces hearing ability in most of us as we approach retirement, although it is often quite gradual. Signs usually emerge when in crowded company and it becomes more difficult to pinpoint individual voices.

There is no cure for this gradual loss of hearing but it can, of course, be counteracted by using one of the modern hearing aids now available either on the NHS or privately. If you are experiencing difficulties do not hesitate to have your ears checked and, if necessary, shop around for what is suitable. Expect to be a little self-conscious when first using a hearing aid, but this will quickly wear off. You might be surprised at how many of your friends and colleagues are using them. Several of the more sophisticated - and more expensive - models cannot be seen at all. In any case, vanity should be overcome in the interests of being able to join in the conversation again.

The Royal National Institute for Deaf People and the British Deaf Association can both help in cases of more severe deafness, the latter offering courses in sign language for the more serious cases.

Tinnitus is different from hearing loss. It is when a near-constant 'ringing' can be heard in the ears or head. Science has moved forward in leaps and bounds in recent years and the British Tinnitus Association will know the latest developments and what can be done for you.

LOOKING AFTER YOUR HEALTH

Sight

Perhaps the most important sense of all, this is one you really must look after. Have your eyes checked at least every two years, and more frequently if you are having difficulty. Seek advice, in particular, as to the type of spectacles best suited to you. Eye tests are free for many people, including those on a low income, diabetics and anyone with glaucoma or a close relative suffering from this disease.

Your eyes are examined not merely to find out how well you can see. Inherent or potential problems can be identified, as can people who may have a related neurological disease. Colour blindness (very common, partially, in men) can be detected; and your eyes are also a mirror for your general state of health. So don't skip these.

Cataracts are not the problem they used to be. Today eight out of ten patients who have this minor operation are discharged the same day. A local anaesthetic is usually sufficient; about 100,000 patients a year are following this route.

Memory

If there is one feature of our everyday lives which supposedly indicates the onset of old age it is an apparent loss of memory. How often have you heard the cry 'I must be getting old - I can't remember where I put anything any more,' or the like?

While studies are continuing, there is increasing evidence that, providing you maintain a reasonable state of health, your memory will not fade. If you feel that it is doing so, it is probably either because you never used to worry about it when you were younger, or your general health has deteriorated. After nearly twenty years of research at Addenbrooke's Hospital, Cambridge, this is the conclusion.

So stay healthy and forget about your memory! It is packed, in any case, with an increasing amount of information as each year passes. Any difficulties you might be experiencing are almost certainly a question of retrieval. The information you want is there somewhere; it may just take a little longer to find.

Some Possible Problems

Stress

Retirement itself, especially if it has come earlier than expected, is stressful until you have re-organised yourself. It remains quite high in Dr. Richard Rahe's Stress Tables (see below). Rahe, an American psychiatrist, drew up a list of events occurring in people's lives. He allocated a number to each (with 100 as the highest) representing the level of stress that event produced in a person. Some of the more common events are listed opposite.

LOOKING AFTER YOUR HEALTH

Life Event	Stress Factor
Death of a spouse	100
Divorce	73
Separation	65
Personal injury/illness	53
Marriage	50
Retirement	45
Pregnancy	40
Business readjustment	39
Job change	36
Moving house	20
Holidays	13
Christmas	12

Stress and relaxation go hand-in-hand, and having too little to do can be every bit as stressful as being too busy. That is why self-organisation is so important, so go back and read Chapter 1 again if necessary!

Teach yourself to relax

Relaxation is a state of mind - and one that many people have to learn how to handle. Classes are available, although a few simple tips are all that you need to succeed. You must teach your brain to cut out everything else (what to have for tea, whether or not to go on that cruise, worrying about young Johnny, and so on) and concentrate on relaxation itself. This will be made easier by selecting a quiet, comfortable spot (it can be your favourite armchair or the middle of a field), wearing light and easy clothing and having no distractions whatsoever.

Get into a relaxed position. Breathe calmly and deeply for a few seconds. Now, slowly, clench your fingers and toes. Then, slowly, unclench them. Similarly, shrug and unshrug your shoulders; bend and unbend your knees and elbows; tighten and contract your face muscles; and finally take three or four very deep breaths. Each should entirely fill your lungs, and exhaling should completely empty them. Do all this at least twice a day, wherever you are.

A booklet of simple exercises approved by physiotherapists for the over-70s costs just £1 from Mrs. Vera Badley(see Help List).

At other times, sit down and read your favourite book or magazine for half an hour; listen with closed eyes to some music you really enjoy or go for a stroll - preferably without the dog!

If the weather is particularly warm, avoid strenuous activity, wear light clothing, make sure your house is well ventilated and drink plenty of liquids other than alcohol.

Sleep

Don't get too hung up about sleep unless it's a real problem, in which case see your doctor - although avoid medication if at all possible. There is no such thing as a 'normal' amount of sleep; we all vary on this score. A nap in the afternoon or early evening may replace some of the sleep you need at night, so be prepared to do other things

LOOKING AFTER YOUR HEALTH

such as reading or listening (quietly!) to music late at night. Coffee will not help you sleep, whatever some folk may say.

Sexual Activity

There are more myths surrounding this subject and ageing than any other, and you should be extremely wary of what you hear or read casually on the topic.

The fact is that everyone's sexual life is personal and individual. No-one knows what is 'average' sexual activity, simply because people who take part in surveys do not always speak the truth. Statistics are thus contaminated, and all that so-called experts can do is to generalise on the subject.

Change, not loss

You, however, know your own activity rates and preferences, and while these might diminish as you run into your 60s and 70s, they will certainly not disappear. If they do, the reason will not be ageing but some other symptom which needs investigating. And don't overlook the initial stress factor of retirement, which may be contributing. You and your partner are probably now spending much more time together, and changing patterns like these can often be temporarily disruptive. Sexual activity need not involve full intercourse every time, and both of you may well be quite satisfied with something less.

If you are still concerned about your sex life, first speak to your doctor - although as most would admit, they are not specialists in this field, and a consultant is more appropriate. Relate (the former Marriage Guidance Council) offers counselling through 130 centres (in Scotland it is Marriage Counselling Scotland), and there are also smaller, privately sponsored organisations in larger cities. Try also The Association of Sexual and Marital Therapists.

Phobias

There is no reason why advancing years should exacerbate any special fears you might have, but you may believe that in older age you will have more difficulty facing up to these. The likelihood is, that while this holds some truth, maturity coupled with a more relaxed attitude to life will act as a counterbalance.

Phobias should not be treated lightly, however, especially by those close to the sufferer. Research as to reasons is thin, but there is no doubting the real fear that, say, flying or spiders produces in some people. In older people agoraphobia (the fear of open spaces and public places) or nosophobia (the fear of becoming ill) should not be ignored if symptoms persist; these two feature in the top ten phobias in the UK.

If you are afflicted, face up to your fears a step at a time, and talk freely to others about them. Provide yourself with a reward as you gradually begin to overcome them. The Phobics Society and Phobic Action are just two bodies that can assist.

LOOKING AFTER YOUR HEALTH

Smoking - for smokers only!

You didn't think you were going to get away without a fuller reference in a chapter on health, did you?

Smoking kills

You already know that smoking is a killer and that we lose no less than 50,000 Britons a year because of it. You probably know that your chances of catching lung cancer are twenty times greater than if you don't smoke. Heart disease, thrombosis and bronchitis are also more likely to get you. A major research project funded by, amongst others, the Medical Research Council, has just discovered that among people in their 70s heart attacks are twice as common for smokers as for non-smokers.

No-one said that giving up was easy but now you have a new opportunity. You can either look forward to another twenty years or so of work-free life - or not. And don't kid yourself that cigars and pipes are OK: they're not.

Give it up

Fix a date now, not too far into the future, when you will enjoy your last puff. On that day dispose of everything associated with smoking - ash-trays, lighters, matches, etc. Commit your intentions to paper and pin it up prominently; tell everyone you are going to do it. And vow not to cadge from friends in the future. If it's really tough, ring Quitline or, in Scotland, Smokeline.

Find substitutes

Ideally, find something to replace smoking - perhaps a sweet you particularly enjoy and haven't tried for years. And remember that smoking affects not only you but those who surround you - and that might include grandchildren. Passive smoking also kills.

Best of luck!

5 EATING FOR HEALTH

- Eat to lose weight
- Foods you can eat more of
- Foods to avoid
- What we drink
- More about weight loss
- Food supplements
- Eating abroad
- Summing up

If there is one thing you can do quite easily to prolong your lifespan, it is to eat sensibly. There are no excuses not to do so and, within reason, your level of income should not prevent you from making careful selections in your grocery store. Boiled potatoes are no more expensive than fatty chips, and fruit and vegetables can easily replace many junk foods without costing you a penny more.

Eat To Lose Weight

People in Britain are getting fatter - and fat kills. No less than one in five of us is obese, according to Government statistics. We are eating out more, and exercising less. Is it any wonder that many of us are carrying around a stone or two (or more!) we could do without?

Getting it off is not easy - don't let's kid ourselves. It's even more difficult in later years, simply because our eating habits will have developed into a pattern, making change less palatable. But, set against this, look what you can gain:

- an improved appearance
- greater confidence in company
- an ability to tackle a host of activities more easily, and - most important of all -
- a longer life.

Strict dieting is discussed in more detail below; here we are merely proposing a healthier eating regime from now on. Vow to start it today - not tomorrow; it never comes. Once you have digested the vital components of healthy eating, as described in this chapter, make a short list of the things *you* need to change in order to introduce a spanking new style of eating into your life. You'll never regret it.

Foods You Can Eat More Of

Fibre

Fibre is the name for a particular group of carbohydrates (a chemical mixture of carbon, hydrogen and oxygen which exists in a host of foodstuffs) that is found only in foods that grow in the ground. So tuck in to things like cereals (except those over-sweetened with added sugar - see below), rice, pasta, beans, peas, vegetables and fruit. And don't forget wholemeal bread.

Helps whole health

Fibre is a healthy addition to your diet in so many different ways. It helps to break up other food which you have consumed and thus does its bit to prevent constipation. It is usually quite filling, but it doesn't weigh in with too many calories. Bowel difficulties such as diverticulitis or haemorrhoids (piles) will be eased with a daily helping of fibrous food. Laxatives should not be necessary if you are taking adequate fibre and, if you are eating enough fruit and vegetables, neither should added fibre such as natural bran, although many people prefer to use this.

Remember also that such diverse complaints as varicose veins and hiatus hernia can be affected by what you eat. Fibre may also help to relieve these painful conditions.

If the fibre argument is new to you, take it easy at first and don't overdo it. Your body needs to adjust itself to any changed eating regime, although it will quickly adapt. Adults are advised to eat at least 30 grams (about 1 oz.) each day. To give you an indication of fibre levels, study the table overleaf:

4 slices wholemeal bread	11 grams
1 serving breakfast cereal	3-5 grams
1 serving wholemeal spaghetti	6 grams
1 serving brown rice	3 grams
1 serving beans or peas	6 grams
1 jacket potato	3 grams
2 dried apricots	7 grams

You can see what is good for you and how to get to that 30 grams a day although there are lots of other choices. Write to the Health Education Authority for their useful booklet on healthy eating.

Fruit and Vegetables

You already know the value of these foodstuffs because of the fibre they contain, but there's more to it than that. Fruit and vegetables also provide us with vitamins and minerals essential for the maintenance of our well-being, and especially Vitamin C which is only found in these items. Soft woodland fruits, bananas and tomatoes are all excellent sources.

There is a general rule which states that the greener the vegetable, the better it is for you, and this certainly applies to deeper green produce such as spinach and darker cabbage. If you are able to eat your fruit and vegetables raw this is even better to avoid cooking away the goodness. The fibre they contain is concentrated in the

EATING FOR HEALTH

skins, or just under them. So eat the whole of your next jacket potato, and don't peel apples and pears unless you have a serious dental problem. Do be sure, though, to wash all fruit and vegetables thoroughly before eating or cooking them.

Fresher the better

Processing removes a lot of vitamins, so avoid canned items if you can. The fresher the foodstuffs are the better. Although frozen fruit and vegetables are nutritious, they still come second best to the original, untouched article eaten as soon as possible after being picked.

The water that you cook your vegetables in will contain a lot of exuded goodness, so use it to make gravy or turn it into broth with - preferably - chicken or turkey carcasses. And as a change from potatoes, try vegetables like pumpkins or squash which can be made into either sweet or savoury dishes. Pumpkin and ginger chutney is delicious!

Organic for you?

Organic - or naturally produced - foods may or may not form part of your diet from today, according to your opinion about the matter. Many feel that there is little research, and thus not a lot of positive proof, that fertilisers and other additives will do you any long-term harm. But if you feel otherwise, then equally, not consuming these items won't hurt you either. A limited variety of organic fruit and vegetables is becoming available in our larger supermarkets. You can probably find more, or track down a local source, at your local health food store. You will also find that organic meats - beef, lamb, pork - and organic dairy products are increasingly available in the shops. All these foods cost slightly more than their non-organic counterparts, but if you feel your health will benefit, it might be worth the extra expense. The choice is yours. A helpful booklet, 'Where to Buy Organic Foods' is published by the Soil Association.

Foods To Avoid

Fat

Fat kills. Make no mistake about it. The more saturated fats you eat, the more cholesterol you are pumping into your bloodstream. This builds up on the inside of your arteries, including those leading to the heart, and when it is dense enough can cause a heart attack. With sensible eating this can be avoided.

Avoid saturated fat

Saturated fats exist in most meats, especially in beef, pork, lamb and other red meats, as well as in milk, cheese, butter, certain vegetable oils and some nuts. It follows that foods made with any of these ingredients will be high in these fats: patès, meat pies and sausages, crisps (cooked in oil), biscuits, milk puddings, ice cream and chocolate to name but a few. Egg yolks, fish roe and shellfish are also high in cholesterol.

EATING FOR HEALTH

Cholesterol is a complex constituent, though, and should not be avoided altogether. Fats should not be completely cut out of your diet (in fact, it would be nearly impossible to do so) but eaten in moderation. Aim at items which contain unsaturated fats and especially those with monounsaturated fat. The most common of these is olive oil, and cooking with this oil is a very healthy choice, especially if you use the 'virgin' form. Oils such as safflower, sunflower and corn oils, which are polyunsaturated, are, according to the latest research, not as healthy a choice as olive oil - although all are better than the really harmful saturated animal fats. Oily fish like fresh tuna and salmon, mackerel, sardines and herring, on the other hand, are another form of 'healthy oil', and are to be heartily recommended.

Cut down in small ways

There are other ways of cutting down on the fat. Grill instead of fry; cut fat from the edges of meat; slice chips (when you are going to treat yourself!) thickly; eat lean mince; drink skimmed or semi-skimmed milk; eat more chicken (but not the skin); spoon fat from gravy after it has stood for a little while; and so on. Not too difficult is it?

If you want to know just how much saturated fat there is in most food items, look at the information on the pack or tin: you will soon become quite an expert!

Sugar

We all eat too much sugar - most of it hidden in other foodstuffs. Did you know that a glass of Coke contains about five teaspoonfuls? Or that there are nine teaspoons' worth in just one Mars bar? Or twenty-two in a five ounce box of liquorice allsorts?

The problem with sugar is that it fills you full with calories - but very little else. There are no vitamins, fibre, minerals, or protein in sugar. If the average weekly consumption were to be cut by half, it would not be enough.

Cut it down

If you are still taking sugar in tea or coffee, now is a good time to give it up. Your drinks will taste dreadful for about two or three weeks; thereafter, you will wonder how you ever drank them with added sugar in the first place!

Look on food labels to see how much sugar you really are consuming. And don't miss out on dextrose, fructose, glucose or sucrose - all these mean sugar as well. You'll find them in the oddest of places, like crisps, cheese

EATING FOR HEALTH

biscuits and other apparent savouries. Brown, raw and cane sugars are just as bad for you; their calorie content is the same as the white variety.

Salt

Another 'hidden' ingredient of nearly all foodstuffs is salt, and while a little of it won't do us a great deal of harm, many of us overdo it. It shouldn't be necessary to add salt at the table to most cooked foods; there is generally enough there already.

Beware particularly of adding salt to soups and main courses simply because your taste buds are less sensitive than they once were. Ask the family what they think, and if the majority of them believe the food to be salty enough already, put the condiments well out of everyone's reach.

Try a substitute

Overindulgence in salt can lead to high blood pressure, which places unnecessary reliance upon the heart. Try one of the many tasty natural herbs or spices on the market as a substitute, and keep away from heavily salted foods such as gammon or salted fish. Try also one of the 'low salts' on the market.

What We Drink

Providing we don't go wild, our bodies will take almost as much non-alcoholic fluid as we care to fill them with. We should not, of course, be swilling a lot of high-sugar content liquids, but certainly water should be drunk regularly, along with any other fluids not harmful to our system.

Water, water

Our kidneys function more efficiently when (a) they have a great deal of liquid to deal with and (b) this is not too concentrated. Water should therefore be drunk in order to dilute whatever else we are taking on board. One of the best ways of avoiding a hangover is to drink as much water as you did alcohol before going to bed. You may have to get up during the night, but you should avoid that headache in the morning!

Tea, coffee, low- or sugar-free soft drinks and beer in moderation will all suffice to keep everything in working order. Coffee, unless decaffeinated, should be drunk only in moderation. Tea, although it contains a little caffeine, is an ideal regular drink - but still in moderation as too much can hinder continence - and will even help you to digest your food. Eighty per cent of Britons drinking 170 million cups a day can't be wrong!

Alcohol

The case for and against alcohol has fluctuated over the years, but the modern view is that a little of what you fancy really does do you good. A recent report entitled 'Drinking to Your Health', published by the Social Affairs Unit, suggests that drinking in moderation has beneficial effects. Alcohol, says the medical profession generally, is only dangerous to the system when taken unwisely.

Moderation

But how much is moderation? The accepted view is that men can drink 21 units a week and women 14 without coming to any harm; even higher levels have been put forward by some researchers. A table of typical unit values appears below. Obviously these units should be spread over the week, and the drinks preferably taken with food. At the same time, it is wise to give your system a complete rest from alcohol for a few days every so often. And of course don't drink and drive.

This is a very general guide, and acceptable intake will vary according to body weight, overall health and regularity of drinking. A small drink late at night can assist peaceful sleep. Much alcohol contains trace elements of zinc, copper, manganese and potassium, as well as Vitamin B, and - believe it or not - all of these (in the correct quantities) can do you good! On the other hand most alcoholic drinks contain calories, so take into account what impact these might have on your weight.

Don't turn to it too often

If you are feeling lonely or depressed you may be tempted to drink more than the suggested levels and, if this is the case, do seek medical advice before it turns into a habit. It is very easy to convince yourself that a few extra drinks are not causing you any harm. The truth is that they probably aren't at that stage, but if you get into a habit they certainly will. Remember, also, that tolerance to alcohol tends to decrease with age.

Two useful guidelines are that (a) drinking should always be enjoyed and (b) you should never really feel the need to have a drink. If you are drinking for the sake of it without enjoying it and sometimes feel in desperation for a drink, then these are warning signs. Seek help.

Typical unit values (in all cases appropriate-size glasses):

A glass of wine, sherry or port	1
A pint of beer or lagerl	2
A small measure of spirits	1 - 1½
A can of strong beer or lager	3

More About Weight Loss

What is a diet? For some, the word will mean a strict regime of eating only certain quantities and types of foods, day in and day out. For others it will amount to nothing more than sensible eating on a regular basis, and this is what you should be aiming for.

EATING FOR HEALTH

Calories

We can't do without calories but we do need to strike a balance between our input and the sort of life we lead. Calories are more correctly known as kilocalories, but the shorter word is accepted world wide - and the 'joule' is also beginning to take over. However we term them, calories provide us with energy, and a boxer therefore needs a great deal more than an office worker.

There are no hard-and-fast figures for the expenditure of calories, simply because the amount you use will depend upon the physical strength and ability of each individual. But there is a simple test which lets you know when you are taking more on board than you are using - you get fatter.

Activities such as swimming, cycling, climbing stairs and even dancing use up a greater number of calories than more sedentary pursuits like bowling or walking. On the other side of the scales, steaks, beer, chocolate and the like will top you up with calories more so than, say, baked beans, bread or cheese. You can see, however, that some of these are also heavy on cholesterol, so a sensible balance has to be maintained.

Places to avoid are our many fast-food outlets, unless you are specifying jacket potatoes, wholemeal rolls and water. Most of the rest of the menu will be high in calorie content. Quarterpounders (ie a quarter of a pound beefburger) typically contain between 400 and 500 calories, and to use these up you would have to do about an hour's worth of cycling or swimming! A whole pizza is no better, incidentally, so although you can spoil yourself on the odd occasion, regular visitors beware.

Find out if you're overweight

You should already know if you are overweight or not. Depending upon sex, height and the size of your body frame there are plenty of guidelines about to keep you advised. Look in any authoritative book, or ask your doctor if you are unsure. Alternatively attend a Weight Watchers 'clinic' and see if you pass the test! Weight Watchers (UK) Ltd. have well over 3,000 groups across the country, there to help you. If you are unable, or unwilling, to attend their meetings, try Weight Watchers by Mail who offer to keep you in trim by post and telephone. The Women's Nutritional Advisory Service also runs a postal course especially for women experiencing weight difficulties associated with the menopause.

Dieting

You should not begin dieting seriously without first of all speaking to your doctor. Many people do not take into account the impact that a major change in food intake can have on their body. You may be advised to diet in stages, so as not to cut out foods which provide basic nutrients.

EATING FOR HEALTH

Cut down on junk food first

Cutting down (or out!) such foods as chocolate biscuits, sweet puddings, crisps and the like needs no advice at all. Do it and see what effect it has on your weight, then you can decide how much further you need to go to achieve your ideal figure. If you have the cash, a visit to a health 'farm' will certainly give you a psychological boost and might even take off a pound or two as well. Forget the carrot juice stories; today's modern health spas have cordon bleu restaurants that will serve you superb, but low calorie, meals.

Once you reach your ideal weight, sensible eating - coupled with adequate exercise - should take care of you in the future. An occasional binge is quite in order providing you take care most of the time!

Food Supplements

Vitamins and tonics

There should normally be no need at these if you are eating a regular, healthy mixture of fruit and vegetables along with your meals. One possible exception could be the need for a tonic on a temporary basis following a prolonged spell of illness, but this should only be on a doctor's advice. Tonics are never a long term remedy.

Fabulous fish oil

All kinds of vitamin pills stand on the shelves of the health shops beckoning us to buy them to build up our resources, but few of them are really necessary. One possible exception is cod liver oil pills, which can help prevent the clogging of arteries. If you don't eat oily fish that often, you might do well to use this supplement.

Gorgeous garlic

Garlic is another additive that can easily be digested by way of capsules (stick to the odourless variety for obvious reasons!), and which doctors agree can help to control cholesterol and thus reduce the risk of heart attack. Just how it does this is still unclear, but numerous trials have pointed to its success. Not only does it help to cut fat levels in the bloodstream, but latest research shows that it also reduces the blood's viscosity and prevents it from clotting.

Apart from these two proven additives (fish oil and garlic), if you believe that a vitamin pill a day is doing you good, it probably won't do you any harm either. But you could be spending your money more wisely!

The humble aspirin

Whilst neither vitamin nor tonic, the humble aspirin is proving vital in saving the lives of heart attack and stroke victims. Professor Richard Peto of Oxford University believes that up to 7,000 lives could be saved every year in the UK if just one small dose (75 mg) of the soluble variety were taken each day by those vulnerable to such attacks.

However, do discuss this first with your doctor to make certain that in your case it is (a) advisable and (b) does not clash with any other medication you may be taking.

Eating Abroad

If you have made your post-retirement home abroad, it may be a little more difficult to keep to a balanced diet, depending upon what local produce is available. But the same rules apply: everything in moderation and a good helping of fruit and vegetables daily.

Substitute the traditional items you are used to at home with something providing equal benefit in terms of proteins. And moderate your alcohol intake even if it is a lot cheaper!

If you are living in warmer climes, drink plenty of water to keep your kidneys functioning properly. Buy bottles if the local variety is questionable. And avoid very hot, spicy foods wherever you are; your own stomach will usually let you know what it will tolerate on this front.

Summing Up

You may, admittedly, be thoroughly confused by now and asking yourself a plethora of questions.

Should I lose weight? Is dieting really necessary? How many calories a day do I need? How much fibre will do me good? Am I drinking too much alcohol - or not enough water? And so on.

As with most things in life, the answer lies in one word - moderation. Try, if at all possible, to eat larger meals towards the beginning and middle of the day, moving on to lighter variations as the day proceeds - not easy given our traditional eating pattern, but you will feel a lot better for it.

Then vary what you eat as much as your budget will allow. Don't get into the habit of sticking to the same meals on certain days of the week. Try to eat more fibre-rich foods and plenty of fresh fruit and vegetables. Eat less fat, sugar and salt. Don't drink any more than the recommended quantities of alcohol.

If you do all this, you can probably have the odd helping of bread pudding while holding to the right weight and feeling better. It's well worth a try.

6 FINDING FRESH INTERESTS

- Back to work
- Hobbies and interests

You may - perhaps - be able to skip this chapter. 'I've already got plenty of interests - I don't need any more', do I hear you say? Yes, but remember that, up until retirement, you might have had at most, say, 15 hours a week in which to pursue those interests. Now you could have another 50 hours or so! Are you sure you really want to spend that long on your current interests, however passionate you may be about them?

You may be looking forward to playing a lot more golf, or bridge. That will still be possible, but it is highly likely you will still be left with 10 or perhaps 20 hours or more each week to fill. If you are determined not to be a lounge lizard, then fresh interests should be attractive to you.

They may even help you prevent colds. According to a recent study of 276 healthy men and women, reported in the Journal of the American Medical Association, those with more social connections were found to be four times less likely to catch a cold than those who mixed less frequently! Researchers are unsure how the protection works but suggest that people with more social ties are motivated to take better care of themselves because these 'networks' promote feelings of self-worth, responsibility, control and meaning in life.

Back To Work

One of your new interests could be a return to work either on a paid or a voluntary basis. We look at voluntary work in Chapter 7. But before deciding on paid work, do consider what your driving force is. The most powerful, of course, will be the need for extra income, but avoid rushing into the first vacancy that falls into your lap. Consider first:

- How many hours a week do I really want to work?
- Will this kind of work still motivate me?
- How far am I prepared to travel daily (remember the winter!)?
- Just how much will I receive after paying tax?

Assuming you are over 55, finding new work will not be easy although there are certain avenues where age can be an advantage. The Corps of Commissionaires is always eager to find reliable ex-servicemen and women, as well as former prison officers, firemen, coastguards and merchant seamen, to fill their posts; temporary work is available until age 70. The government can also help through its Restart Programme: visit your local Jobcentre.

FINDING FRESH INTERESTS

If you own a personal computer and enjoy operating it, you could become a 'flexi-worker' without leaving the comfort of your home. Home-working is becoming very popular; look out for appropriate advertisements or contact BT or Mercury Communications.

Whatever job you may be seeking, the first thing you have to do is to sell yourself and that you will achieve through a good curriculum vitae (CV). Remember that this is the first 'picture' of you that a prospective employer receives. Make sure he gets the right image - one that you would like to give.

Your own business

Starting your own business demands a lot of careful consideration and was referred to briefly in Chapter 2; take bags of advice and plenty of time before jumping into this particular pool. You might though - if you've £50,000 or more of surplus savings (ie beyond what you actually require) - consider becoming a Business Angel and investing in a company where you can have some influence (although not normally control). Speak to one of the major accountancy firms and subscribe to 'Business Money Facts' but remember this is a high risk alternative.

Hobbies And Interests

But let's move to hobbies and interests and take a look at a selection of these. First, though, if you are moving into new territory there are three factors to think about before going too far. The first must be cost: while it might appear attractive, for instance, to learn to fly, it's going to be expensive. There's also the fact that after qualifying, you could be tempted into buying a stake in an aeroplane! So think ahead.

The other two considerations are how much time your new interest is likely to occupy (you don't want it taking over other already well-established hobbies), and what impact it might have upon your partner and/or other members of your family. Learning to play the trumpet could fall into this last category! All three of these points should be given ample thought before proceeding.

What then is available? To say that the possibilities are limitless would not be an exaggeration. You only have to visit your local main library to see what is on offer - everything from aerobics to zoology and all the letters in-between.

Further education

Let's start by taking a look at what might be on offer at your local college. All the usual tuition will be available but what about trying something completely different - tracing ancestors, field archaeology, advanced driving, lip reading, fashion design - or even self-defence if you're feeling strong enough! Unless you really live in the wilds, there will be a centre of learning within striking distance, at least once a week. Adult education is not what it was: it's more exciting and offers hundreds of possibilities at minimal cost for those with time on their hands. You can even work your way into University through an Access

FINDING FRESH INTERESTS

programme over one or two years; these courses are recognised nationally and after successful completion students qualify for entry into higher education.

If you're really prepared to knuckle down, the Open University has courses consisting of a mix of correspondence work, cassettes and radio or television programmes, and quite often residential schools. The speed at which you study is entirely up to you and a full-credit degree could cost as little as £500 spread over six or seven years. The oldest graduate so far has been a lady of 92!

If studying at home appeals to you, write to the Council for the Accreditation of Correspondence Colleges for advice and a list of authorised colleges. One of these is the National Extension College which offers over 150 courses and is a non-profitmaking body.

We have already said that the list of hobbies and interests available to you has no end, but the following are a few you might like to think about. They have been especially selected as being of interest to those in retirement.

The arts

These may already feature in your lifestyle, but now you have the wonderful opportunity to spend even more time visiting the theatre, ballet, opera, cinema, art gallery or whatever takes your fancy, although obviously within your new budget. You may even indirectly be a National Lottery winner if your particular interest qualifies for a grant and tickets are subsequently cheaper!

If this is a completely new world for you, make contact with your local Arts Board listed in your telephone directory; for those living in Scotland, Wales or Northern Ireland it is your own Arts Council. All of these organise a variety of events throughout the year.

You might like to join the Royal Society for Arts (more correctly The Royal Society for the Encouragement of Arts, Manufactures and Commerce) which provides an independent forum for people from a wide variety of backgrounds. Or perhaps one of the many more esoteric societies devoted to a particular artist or writer - there's even an Agatha Christie Society, run by her grandson!

Film buffs should query the British Film Institute for their local society. And if radio or television switches you on and you would like to be part of an invited studio audience, the BBC Ticket Units would like to hear from you.

Collecting

This is a catch-all title for a habit which very few of us avoid even if it's only commemorative plates, miniature hippopotami or the thimbles which adorn our walls and shelves.

Collecting is a dual-interest hobby in that, apart from the joy in owning the objects themselves, many collectors also become experts in their own subject. This can lead to interesting conversations and, if you gain sufficient authority, to being asked to talk publicly about your collection. In time this might even improve your cash flow!

FINDING FRESH INTERESTS

What you collect is a matter for you alone but be influenced more by your interest in the subject than for any possible investment value. Just ask a few philatelists how the value of their portfolio has risen - and fallen - over the years. Three very popular collecting items are represented by the British Association of Numismatic Societies, the British Model Soldier Society and the National Philatelic Society, each of which will help you to start up.

Antique collecting could be a little more costly but if this appeals select your class of item and study its form before branching out. Visit antique fairs, held across the country; consider joining the Antique Collectors Club; and treat yourself to one of the many guides available in the bookshops. Probably one of the Miller guides will prove the most readable and may well take you into worlds you had not previously imagined.

Conservation

This now has wide appeal and, as an interest, has the added benefit that you spend a great deal of time in the fresh air and so keep healthy into the bargain. Hundreds of clubs and societies exist across the kingdom to preserve and encourage interest in everything from bees to the flowers which serve them, and from canals to whales.

Volunteers are constantly sought and any help you can provide will instantly be accepted with gratitude. Even if you know absolutely nothing about your chosen subject, that will not matter to the enthusiasts; they will be more than keen to teach you and show you the ropes. Field study courses take place every weekend of the year somewhere or other, and are complemented by talks, films and visits.

Contact the Civic Trust, the Forestry Commission, the Wildlife Trusts, or the Countryside Commission - and that's just for starters!

Crafts

This is another interest which has spawned thousands of specialist books and we can only consider it briefly here. The word 'craft' tends to indicate something made by hand (with perhaps the help of a machine), generally at home or in a small workshop. Crafts incorporate a multitude of items ranging from home-cooked goodies to toys, from baskets to lacework, and well beyond.

Skill is clearly needed and if you haven't got it, forget it! But if you would like to develop inherent skills and find out where craft courses throughout the country are held write to the Crafts Council. They can also tell you about craft fairs and markets, and where to obtain materials.

Dancing

This activity, like conservation, will also help you to keep fit - but indoors!

Dancing has seen a comeback in recent years and several leading hotels have even dusted off their palm courts and brought back 'old-time' orchestras and tea dances to cope with the demand. A variety of techniques is available

FINDING FRESH INTERESTS

including ballroom, old time, folk, Scottish, and even disco dancing which has many 60-plus adherents. What's on can usually be found in your local newspaper, or your library may be able to assist.

The British Council of Ballroom Dancing is the governing body for its speciality in this country and will send you a free list of over 300 recognised dance schools. For folk dancing try the English Folk Dance and Song Society or, in Scotland, the Royal Scottish Country Dance Society. There are over 600 folk dance clubs in England alone and these include the famous morris dancers and the cloggers. The Scottish Society publishes its own music and holds a summer school each year in Edinburgh.

Gardening

You may, of course, see this as a chore. But for thousands of people the opportunity to spend even more time in their beloved flower or vegetable patches is an added bonus of retirement - and it keeps you fit. It has been calculated that even gentle gardening burns off more than twice as much fat as walking does, so fish out that trowel and hoe now!

Anything from a window box to a full-blown acre or more counts as gardening and, certainly in the summer months, can occupy as much time as you are prepared to give to it. Along with this interest can go visits to other gardens and garden centres (leave your wallet behind!), reading some of the dozens of gardening magazines regularly, exhibiting at flower or vegetable shows and joining your local horticultural society. So you could let this particular hobby take over your life if that is your desire. And teaching grandchildren to raise their own plants merely adds to the pleasure.

The Royal Horticultural Society, which administers the annual Chelsea Flower Show, is the gardener's 'bible club' and the subscription cost can quickly be recouped if you are a regular garden visitor. If you think you would like to add your own plot, however tiny, to those visited, write to the National Gardens Scheme; it already has 3,500 private gardens available to the public. Similarly, in Scotland, Scotland's Gardens Scheme has over 300 such gardens. Joining a group to visit gardens can be fun and this is what The Garden Studio does, whose trips include exotic destinations like Madeira.

Horticultural Therapy is a wonderful scheme which operates a round-the-clock telephone service for visually impaired people to help them run their own garden.

If you're really proud of your garden, and particularly if it contains valuable plants or statuary, check that your house contents policy includes adequate cover. If it does not, speak to your insurer about this. Garden theft is on the increase and even newly-laid lawns have been known to disappear overnight!

Music

You may already be an avid follower and have read the Arts section above, but have you considered reviving or initiating an interest in playing a musical instrument?

FINDING FRESH INTERESTS

The availability of modestly-priced electronic organs has brought new pleasure to thousands and they really are easier to play than a piano. Lessons can be arranged, and the multitudinous mixture of sounds you can create can be very satisfying indeed. Don't forget the family (and neighbours!) though, and consider buying a pair of earphones to keep complaints to a minimum!

For something different try handbell ringing, and speak to the Handbell Ringers of Great Britain about it. Or go back to your schooldays and treat yourself to a new recorder: the Society of Recorder Players does not provide tuition but will put you in touch with your local group.

If you just want to sing along with your old-time favourites, several companies are reissuing nostalgic cassettes and compact disks; amongst them the appropriately named 'As Time Goes By'.

Painting

You only have to visit your library to discover just how many pensioners have taken up the brush or chalk when local artists exhibit their work. If you feel you have the gift, give it a try - and if you have never tried, do so now. You could be pleasantly surprised with your own results.

There will almost certainly be a group in your area and your library will have details, but don't be afraid of starting one if there is a vacuum locally. Classes are held at most colleges or, alternatively, make contact with the Open College of the Arts, affiliated to the Open University. It offers courses in painting as well as art and design, textiles, interior design, drawing, sculpture and related subjects. Courses can be started at any time and can lead to recognised awards.

Pets

Unless you are travelling regularly, retirement is perhaps the best time of your life to properly take care of and enjoy a pet. They are able to demand more of your attention and at the same time provide companionship, especially if you are alone. But certain pets can also be demanding - if a dog is your first choice, a poodle will not require quite as much exercise as a Great Dane!

Apart from the obvious choices, a number of less common animals and birds can be seen at your pet shop, including hamsters, gerbils, budgerigars - and even a rat (yes, honestly!). Any one can provide hours of amusement without making too many demands on your time and purse.

Take 'kennelling' costs into account (unless you have willing family or friends who can stand in) if you are anticipating regular holidays. If an emergency occurs, such as an unexpected hospitalisation, try the Cinnamon Trust or, in Scotland, Pet Fostering Service Scotland for guidance and help.

Consider a pet-sitting service when you are away from home; see Chapter 9.

Should you be unfortunate enough to lose your pet there is a national network of over 200 volunteers who work to reunite pet owners with lost pets. Ring Petsearch.

FINDING FRESH INTERESTS

Photography

You will either favour the 'idiot-proof' variety of camera or be prepared to drag along a case full of lenses, but in either event this particular interest will get you out and about and at the same time create levels of interest elsewhere. Taking pictures of churches, for example, can lead you to architectural studies; horses to Stubbs' paintings; or athletics meetings to statistics.

You can spend as much or as little as you please and even expensive cameras and ancillary equipment can be bought for a fraction of their original price when second-hand. Deal only with a reputable outlet.

Clubs and societies exist everywhere, and most welcome beginners and experts alike. Again, your local library will assist in tracking these down.

Reading

You may welcome having more time to read, or, if ploughing through swathes of reports formed part of your job, feel you never want to see the printed word again! In either case, you should not miss out on what is so freely available (literally, in the case of libraries) today.

Get to know your library, especially the reference section where whole new worlds may be discovered. Dip into 'The Reader's Encyclopedia' by William Rose Benet to see the variety of authors' works available, and try some of those unfamiliar to you. Browse for hours in bookshops (no-one will pester you!) and visit Hay-on-Wye, the village with more second-hand bookshops than anywhere else in the world. For a few pounds you could come away with twelve months reading!

The Poetry Society exists for those keen to read, write or listen to poetry, and will even assess your own efforts for a small fee. You would be surprised just how many people have a shot at writing their own poems, even if they remain somewhat coy about it at the time.

Bibliophile Books has over 1600 titles in stock available to pensioners at half price or less.

Sport

This includes everything from angling (generally, for coarse fishermen at least, somewhat sedentary) to cycling and swimming, two activities at the top of the exercise list. This aspect of sport was more fully covered in Chapter 4; here we will browse through a few of the possibilities open to you now that you have extra hours in the day.

You may, of course, spectate or participate (or both) but only you can dictate your choice of sport; it really does have to be something in which you are deeply interested. When it becomes a bore to go along, that is the time to change to something fresh; it is important that both your body and your mind are stimulated.

What you will find, now that you can select your timing, is that the river - or the gymnasium, the track, the pool, etc - are far less crowded than at weekends or in the evenings. Queuing should be a thing of the past, and many activities become so much more pleasant.

FINDING FRESH INTERESTS

Among those sports appealing to the older person are bowling, tennis, swimming, archery and (although it only just qualifies as a 'sport'!) rambling. Find out what's going on in your neighbourhood and join the gang!

Writing

This interest, as this author can assure you, is every bit as stimulating as others although it's not the best way of trying to keep fit!

It is said that everyone has a novel in them, but putting that into words that will sell is another story. Despite this, many thousands of people across the country regularly put pen to paper and produce novels, short stories, articles and poems (see also Reading above), the vast majority of which never reach publication. The market is a tough one and for every article published by any popular women's magazine, for instance, well over one hundred are discarded. But don't be put off if you feel creative; writing can be one of the most satisfying of all hobbies, and not everyone wants to make money out of it.

Most larger towns and cities have Writers' Circles or Workshops (back to the library) and these are aimed at novices as well as established authors. Nearly all are dominated by people with full-time jobs or who are retired, and who write a few lines now and again. Advice and encouragement are available a-plenty so don't be afraid of going along.

Seminars, half- and one-day courses, and week-long residential courses are held all over the place throughout the year; 'Writers News', which also runs home study courses, will provide you with details. Books on the art of writing can be counted in their hundreds as a visit to your bookshop will show. A & C Black and Allison and Busby both specialise in these.

If you're disabled

Those with a handicap need not be excluded from the vast majority of the above activities, and increasingly efforts are being made to improve access and facilities to meet their needs. Some of the following might be useful, although there are of course numerous other specialised bodies which exist to help those with specific disabilities:

- The National Association of Disablement Information and Advice Services.
- Royal Association for Disability and Rehabilitation.
- Motability.
- RNIB Talking Book Service.

7 HELPING IN THE COMMUNITY

- Suit yourself
- A world of choice

You could, if you so wished, spend all of your time helping out in the voluntary sector. There is such a wide variety of organisations crying out for help that it can be difficult to make a choice. It is wise, then, to lay down a few criteria before reaching a final decision. This way you can avoid committing yourself to something which, later, might turn out to be unsatisfying. At that stage it can be a little embarrassing to withdraw.

Suit Yourself

Ask yourself precisely what kind of work appeals mostly to you. Could you, for instance, work with those who have committed crimes - or would you find it too harrowing? Would coping with handicapped people prove too strenuous? Or might you find trying to help the sick rather distressing? Be honest with your feelings at this stage; it's far better to draw out your likes and dislikes now rather than later.

Decide also how many hours each week you are able, or prepared, to spend on this aspect of your life. What will happen when you go away on holiday? Is there a rota system in operation that will allow you to change shifts from time to time to fit in with your diary?

Once you have laid down your basic 'requirements', study this chapter to see into which category they best fall. Then check to see that these activities exist in your own area; travelling anything beyond fifteen minutes or so each way may turn a treat into a chore, although some tolerance may be necessary if you live deep in the countryside.

A World Of Choice

Look in Yellow Pages or under 'Voluntary' or 'Volunteer' in your telephone directory, and ask also at your library, Jobcentre or Citizens' Advice Bureau to check what is in demand in your locality. There will certainly be no shortage.

Helping each other

Perhaps the most obvious area in which to offer your assistance is in helping older people - even if you are barely older, or the same chronological age as those you are helping!

Some people do seem to get older more quickly than others, and, as someone once said, age is merely a number on a birth certificate. You are truly as old as you

HELPING IN THE COMMUNITY

feel, and if you would like to give some of your time to those somewhat older (or perhaps feebler) than yourself, there is a great deal out there waiting for you. Look first at family, friends and neighbours; is there someone who could do with a little cheering up from time to time?

Contact the Elderly has over 4,000 volunteers on its books. They visit the housebound, and usually take them out to tea in a group of ten or so once a month at one of the helpers' homes. This way each volunteer's commitment can be limited to providing just one tea a year. Drivers are always in demand, and there is almost certainly a group operating near you, or they will help you to start one locally.

Help the Aged also seeks volunteers, either to work in its High Street shops (see later under Charity Shops), or with administration, or developing ideas for raising funds.

Age Concern operates in a similar manner but also offers help with gardening, decorating, organising holidays, operating meals-on-wheels and shopping trips. Over a quarter of a million people (many of them retired) help in this way but additional volunteers are always required.

Helping the sick

There could be no better calling than giving assistance to those who are ill. Numerous ways exist to get in touch with a labyrinth of bodies operating in this field.

The British Red Cross is one of the better known. It has no less than 1,200 centres in the UK offering help to the sick, handicapped, housebound and those convalescing, no matter what age they are. Training is provided for those without previous experience. Equally well known is the Women's Royal Voluntary Service, looking after the needy and providing them with meals, help with shopping, transport and so on. No special qualifications or experience are needed and both men and women helpers are taken on.

Visiting patients in hospital can be very rewarding, and the National Association of Leagues of Hospital Friends will put you in touch with a suitable one. There are over 1,100 autonomous groups, each varying in the way it works but all providing succour and companionship for those in hospital, whether they are in for a short duration or a long one. For those terminally ill the Help the Hospices organisation will welcome your assistance and will put you in touch with a local group.

If you feel you would like to help in a specific, rather than a general, charitable area, then make contact with the appropriate body. You will find volunteers are always wanted. Some of the larger specialised groups are:

- British Heart Foundation
- Cancer Research Campaign
- Imperial Cancer Research Fund
- Leonard Cheshire Foundation
- National Association for Mental Health
- National Back Pain Association
- Royal National Institute for the Blind

HELPING IN THE COMMUNITY

And don't rule out being a blood donor if you are not yet 60. Regular donors may continue giving until they reach 65. Look in the local telephone book for the number of your National Blood Service.

Young people

If there is one surefire way of combating old age, it is working with young children. Ask any volunteer and he or she will quickly assure you that giving guidance to youngsters tends to knock years off your age. This applies just as much to working with toddlers as it does to helping your local scout or guide group - and even more so when you are dealing with the mentally or physically handicapped.

You may feel you are far too 'old' to join in activities of this nature, and it may well be that leading a youth group is best left to younger people. But part-time assistance is another thing, and the occasional talk or example set by someone who has done it all before can be very educational for both parties. Examining for badge tests, for example, is one clear instance where people with experience are needed. And if you have excelled at a sport, what about a spot of coaching at the weekends?

Save the Children is one of the best known bodies in the charitable sector, and it has over 800 branches throughout the country where fund-raising activities take place. Barnardo's (formerly Dr. Barnardo's) is equally well known and whilst it no longer runs care homes, it is still heavily involved with day care centres, playgroups and holiday schemes. Either of these bodies will be delighted to hear from you.

The Children's Society supports young people and families in need whatever their difficulties, and probably operates through your local church. It runs some 120 projects for the groups it helps. If you feel you can cope with youngsters in ill-health, then Action for Sick Children will put you in touch with your local branch, as will the National Children's Home which runs residential children's homes and day care centres.

Scout, Cub-Scout, Brownie and Guide packs and troops exist everywhere, often attached to a church. They will certainly provide an interest, particularly if you feel the urge to put something back into an organisation you were a part of long ago. And if you remember youth club days with pleasure, make contact with Youth Clubs UK, the umbrella body for over 700,000 youngsters who badly need volunteer helpers in all areas.

HELPING IN THE COMMUNITY

Counselling

This is obviously a specialised field, but one that anyone with intelligence and feeling can soon ease themselves into following a period of training - which most of the voluntary bodies provide.

You may care to find out more about the Samaritans or the Citizens' Advice Bureau, both well versed in helping people to face up to life's challenges. Samaritans provides a 24-hour telephone service to those in distress, whilst the CAB (to be found in your local telephone directory) works with over 15,000 volunteers advising callers on everything from social security benefits to where to find a plumber. The Samaritans expect a minimum of three hours a week, whilst the CAB requirement is normally six.

Community Service Volunteers runs a scheme especially for those aged over 50 seeking to be involved in their local community. Help of all kinds is provided to both old and young alike.

Prison visitors are always welcomed if you have an institution in your vicinity. Victim Support operates over 350 groups providing emotional support to those who have suffered from a crime. On the other side of the coin, the National Association for the Care and Resettlement of Offenders offers voluntary work assisting young offenders, as well as training adults who are experiencing difficulty in finding employment following a spell in prison.

Public and political

These are grouped together as they tend to attract the former manager or senior executive who can often continue to offer his or her expertise into retirement, sometimes on a paid basis.

All of the political parties seek voluntary help, especially when local and national elections fall due and this might involve anything from envelope-stuffing to driving the housebound to the polling station. You will find the contact points in your telephone directory.

If you feel able to offer an expert opinion on a particular topic, the Public Appointments Unit is happy to consider your application. And 3i's Independent Director Programme and Jamieson, Scott and Prowess both look for people who, generally, have run their own businesses and are prepared to give their advice to others still doing so. There is naturally a regular commitment in all these posts, some of which are paid.

Business in the Community also seeks people with professional skills who can give guidance to new businessmen and women in their local catchment area. It is an umbrella organisation catering for the many Enterprise Agencies and Trusts dotted around the country, and you would be expected to give at least a day a week, for which a fee may be recoverable.

Many former managers also find new outlets following retirement through the Retired Executives' Action Clearing House, which pinpoints voluntary work, with expenses covered, in your locality. This is run on an entirely free

HELPING IN THE COMMUNITY

basis for both parties involved and has placed thousands of former specialists in voluntary positions for as many hours a week as they wish, giving them a new lease of life.

Finally on the managerial front, you may find a suitable opening with the National Health Service Executive as a non-executive director on one of their many District Health Authorities or Community Trusts. Two or three days a month will be expected of you and the current salary is £5,000 per annum. You will find your local Executive in your telephone directory.

The arts

Voluntary work is available within local amateur dramatic and repertory groups and, even if you have never been involved before in anything like this kind of activity, do consider it for all the fun it can bring.

You don't have to be able to act or sing; scene-shifters, painters, electricians and costume workers are all in demand and, initially at least, amateur experience will suffice. You will quickly become an expert!

The Arts Council of England supports all manner of projects, usually at local arts centres, and, again, you do not have to be 'arty' or 'crafty' to join in. Administrators, book-keepers, lighting men and the like are all on the 'payroll' - except there is no pay!

MAKE THE MOST OF YOUR RETIREMENT

Conservation

This is an increasingly popular area, and there is a continuing demand for people ready to assist in such diverse tasks as dredging canals, propping up ancient buildings, bringing pressure to bear in influential quarters and - if you feel less energetic - making tea and coffee for the others!

Watchdogs are wanted by the Council for the Protection of Rural England to report local threats to the environment, whilst the British Trust for Conservation Volunteers helps to improve the countryside through tree-planting, pond cleaning and footpath restoring. It has a network of over 1,500 local branches and almost certainly operates in your area. Also operating in the countryside is the Ramblers' Association, which can offer you a combination of a hobby and keeping fit. It is not merely a body for walkers but takes care of our legal footpaths at the same time.

Perhaps the best known protector of our heritage is the National Trust, which has an army of volunteers looking after the many historic buildings and other properties which it administers on our behalf. Help is always needed.

If you are into ancient buildings, try either the Society for the Protection of Ancient Buildings or the Council for British Archaeology. The former has a few vacancies for specialised volunteers to work on specific buildings, whilst the latter helps to dig up old ones! No training is necessary for archaeological work, but you do need a strong constitution.

HELPING IN THE COMMUNITY

Two well-known pressure groups always willing to add to their numbers are Greenpeace and Friends of the Earth. Greenpeace looks for local help to raise much-needed funds for its international activities, and Friends of the Earth has a similar need which it achieves through over 250 local groups. In Scotland, the Scottish Conservation Projects Trust looks after the local countryside in the same way that English groups do, and runs Action Breaks when people of like minds get together to put up fences and generally improve the habitat.

Animals

You will either be an animal lover or not; now is probably not the time to change. But if you are attracted to, say, horses, dogs, cats or even monkeys, then there is an organisation for you.

Best known in this country is the Royal Society for the Prevention of Cruelty to Animals. Fundraisers are always needed, as indeed they are by every animal sanctuary whatever their speciality. These include:

- The Monkey Sanctuary (Looe, Cornwall)
- Redwings Horse and Donkey Sanctuary (Frettenham, Norwich)
- Birmingham Dogs Home
- Wood Green Animal Shelters (Wood Green, London; Heydon, Herts; and Godmanchester, Cambridge), and many others.

If you disagree with vivisection, the British Union for the Abolition of Vivisection will be glad to hear from you, and so will the Whale and Dolphin Conservation Society if you believe that these animals should be saved for posterity. Pro-Dogs and the National Canine Defence League cater especially for dogs.

For more specialised interests, there is the British Beekeepers' Association, Chickens' Lib (dedicated to the abolition of battery cages), Lynx (campaigning against the fur trade) and hundreds of others.

Charity shops

I have already mentioned the fundraising activities of many charities with High Street shops. Such outfits have come up in the world since the early days of short-term leases of empty premises. Now, windows are professionally designed, and teams of helpers organised on a roster basis raise millions of pounds a year. So much so that commercial High Street businesses have recently complained of the unfair advantage given such organisations! If you would like to be part of this success story, and the companionship it can bring, just pop into any of the charity shops near you and offer your services. Alternatively, if you have a favourite charity which uses this method of raising money, select your own and make contact with the team. You can usually put in as many - or as few - hours each week as you can afford, and rotas tend to be fairly flexible. No previous selling experience is necessary, and you will quickly learn the value of second-hand (or nearly new!) items ranging from books, ornaments and nic-nacs to clothing of all sorts.

HELPING IN THE COMMUNITY

Helping overseas

Many people who retire in their fifties are finding new horizons overseas through one of the agencies which arranges help for those less able to help themselves, especially in third world countries. Travel costs are normally paid plus an allowance to cover basic living - although don't expect conditions to be like home.

Special skills are sometimes required such as nursing, building, engineering or knowledge of agriculture. If there are two of you able to combine such proficiencies, you are more likely to find a placement easily. Doctor and nurse couples are especially popular, and Africa, Asia and the Caribbean countries are favourite destinations.

Voluntary Service Overseas is one of the largest operators in this field; it places about a thousand volunteers every year, usually for two-year spells. If this is too long a commitment for you, consider the British Executive Service Overseas, which looks for volunteers for projects lasting from a few weeks to about six months. Men and women with professional or technical skills are needed as advisers, and a spouse unable to offer a speciality may accompany you.

The United Nations operates an International Service for people with similar skills, plus either language expertise or the ability to learn quickly. The International Voluntary Service is yet another body seeking volunteers able to teach various crafts. They are happy to take you up to the age of 65, as will Skillshare Africa - whose title says it all.

8 IT'S A COMPUTER WORLD

- Choosing what's right for you
- Printers
- Software
- Add-ons
- The Internet
- Ten golden rules

You might be asking yourself what a chapter on computing is doing in a book about retirement; but did you know that the acquisition of personal computers (PCs) - especially by older people - is the fastest growing interest in the UK? People are not buying computers for their own sake, but for what they can do with them.

Whether you're a golfer, a football enthusiast, a follower of the stock market, a keen gardener, a writer of poems - or whatever - a personal computer can bring new vistas to your favourite pursuit. Do you want to learn a new language? Play chess with an expert? Redesign your house or garden? Create a family tree? Delve into the life of Mozart, or a hundred other composers? Or have instant

IT'S A COMPUTER WORLD

access to an encyclopaedia whose drawings will come alive on screen and include sound effects? All are possible with a PC.

And on top of all this you can, if you wish and for very little extra cost, link up to some 50 million other personal computer users across the world, and share common interests by 'talking' to them.

If you are already an addict - and many of the newly converted who are buying PCs are in the age 50-plus bracket - you probably don't need to read on. But if you have never given the purchase of a computer any thought before, do so now. And rest assured that even if your current knowledge of the subject is a big nil, within a couple of months you will find yourself in a completely new and inspiring world. No technical knowledge at all is necessary and you do not need to know how to type.

There are some very good general guidebooks available in the stores and you might like to find one that suits you. Most of them assume that you know absolutely nothing about the subject; there are even 'Idiot's Guides'! The major computer retailers also run training courses for beginners.

Choosing What's Right For You

This is not a computer book, but if your interest has now been whetted you will want to know something about the different kinds of PCs on the market and what is likely to be the most suitable for you.

MAKE THE MOST OF YOUR RETIREMENT

Without dismissing the Apple Macintosh which has a system all of its own, you are probably going to find it easier to stick with the industry standard, ie an 'IBM compatible' machine. This operates using a system known as Windows ('95' is the latest version and '98' will soon take its place).

The 'hardware' are the bits and pieces you use, ie the computer itself, the screen and the keyboard. Printers, also hardware, are normally sold separately and are dealt with below.

There are basically five different ways in which you might use your personal computer:

- As a word processor, to write letters, stories, poems, reports, diaries, etc.

- As a drawing and colouring medium for producing cards, posters, notices, banners and so on.

- For 'spreadsheets', ie for horizontal and/or vertical columns of figures needed to run your accounts, insurance details, your investment portfolio or keeping price records.

- A database for maintaining names and addresses, telephone numbers, club membership names and details, or even recipes.

- A communications post if you decide - later on - to join the network of other users. You can also send others 'e (electronic)-mail' or faxes with this add-on.

IT'S A COMPUTER WORLD

Printers

Sometimes you will be offered a particular printer as part of a package, but more normally these are sold separately.

Price is a good indicator of what you will get, since the market is highly competitive. You will need to decide at the outset whether black and white printing will suffice or whether you require colour. Almost certainly if you get hooked you will want to add colour to your productions, whatever they are. And your grandchildren will certainly expect it as a matter of course!

Software

Word processors

A word processor is the modern term for what we all know as a typewriter, except that it can do hundreds of little extra jobs for us that typewriters can't cope with such as checking our spelling, providing us with alternative words (a thesaurus), tidying up what we are writing and many otherwise tedious tasks. And it's really no more difficult to master.

You don't have to be able to type, as we have already said. Two-finger typing will produce quite fast speeds which most people find adequate for their needs. But you could always pop into a typing school to become a little faster if you feel like it; courses usually last around three months and are not expensive.

Word processing is the program (American spelling is used for this word!) you will use for producing letters, notes, simple records (there is a database version for comprehensive or longer types), diaries and similar straightforward documents. You can correct mistakes as you go along (throw away your eraser!), underline words or quote them in bold type, count how many words you have typed, change the layouts, produce items in various kinds of fonts (lettering) or sizes and even insert pictures if you want to. Nothing could be so easy once you get the hang of it.

Business and professional

Hundreds of programs also exist to take care of practically anything you want to keep in a tidy state. Records of friends' and relatives' names, addresses and telephone numbers, for example (at Christmas time you can print labels or envelopes of all of these to save you hours of work). Or you might want to keep track of your bank accounts or other investments, including detailed items such as stocks and shares. Or your tax returns.

Specialist programs cater for most needs. If you want to keep records of birds spotted, that can easily be done. Club membership records are also no problem. A recipe database (allowing copies of individual items to be printed off as friends seek them!) is easy. And even train buffs are not forgotten; they can keep their records on computer

IT'S A COMPUTER WORLD

which will instantly throw up details of particular locomotives and tell them whether or not they have already been spotted!

Educational

The millions of facts contained in encyclopaedias have now been converted to CD-ROMs (compact disks with a 'read-only memory' which only the manufacturer can 'write' on to prevent you from obliterating anything). If you have seen one of the smaller floppy disks which computers use, you might be amazed to learn that one CD-ROM is equivalent to 450 of these, and yet costs just a few pennies for the manufacturing process. It is this technology that is making computers available to the millions.

Computer versions of encyclopaedias come with moving pictures and sounds and it is these features that attract the young. Ask your grandchildren to show you how to use one!

Also available on disk are full-blown dictionaries, history books, stories of ancient lands and extinct animals, entire art galleries (including the Louvre), atlases, language programs and hundreds of others to keep you (and your family) entertained and educated for as many hours as you can spare.

Entertainment

If you just want to cut yourself off for a few hours from any stresses which remain, try one of the entertainment programs.

You could amuse yourself with clips of bygone comedians, watch almost every spectator sport under the sun, listen to classical (or any other) music whilst you are using your computer for something else, or play a multitude of games from scrabble through noughts and crosses to chess.

But you'll probably have to wait your turn in the queue!

Add-Ons

You may have bought a multi-media computer in the first place, in which case you will already have the ability to see video clips on your monitor and hear the sounds which go with them. Or play musical CDs whilst you are computing.

You may eventually, though, want to go that one step further and add, say, a telephone or a facsimile (fax) link to your machine. With these capabilities you can then instruct your computer to telephone a friend, or send him or her an e-mail or faxed message anywhere in the world for the price of a local telephone call.

The Internet

If you haven't heard of the Internet yet, you will soon do so. It is the world-wide communications network set to revolutionise the way in which we do many of the things we have always taken for granted.

IT'S A COMPUTER WORLD

If you have a modern computer, all you have to do to join is buy yourself a modestly priced modem and appropriate software and, for a few pounds a month, you will be in touch with around 50 million other users from Aberdeen to Zululand. You can then tap in to a wealth of information on almost every subject known to man.

A world of information

You will not need to buy newspapers any more; they will be available on your screen. Entertainment guides will tell you what is on at your local cinema and give details of other events across the country. Railway timetables and AA Roadwatch messages will be available to you at the touch of a button. Shopping could become superfluous: W H Smith, Dixons, Virgin Megastores, Interflora and many others have already put their goods lists on screen. Just click on your requirements and they will be delivered to you, probably next day. You can even see details of houses for sale on screen.

You can link in to the White House (and hear the President's cat, Socks, meow!); call up travel agencies to see what holidays are on offer; or virtually walk around a famous art gallery, with the pictures flashing up before you. Weather news, anywhere in the world, can be called up instantly.

Then you can make contact with someone with your own interests. They may live on the other side of the world but you can 'write letters' to each other which can be instantly read. Even add 'expressions' to letters with certain, recognised symbols.

MAKE THE MOST OF YOUR RETIREMENT

Internet Elders is a world-wide group of people who chat to each other via e-mail. Log in on patd@Chatback.demon.co.uk

There's no end to it once you start.

Ten Golden Rules

If you're the kind of person who studies a subject thoroughly before delving financially into it, you may find yourself bamboozled by the information that is available on computers. Stay sane by remembering - and sticking to - just ten golden rules:

- Before buying any hardware, make a list of the ways in which you might expect to use a computer; you will discover more as you conduct your research.
- Only deal with a reputable dealer and preferably one you can look in the face.
- Ask for a demonstration and use the keyboard yourself.
- Don't be persuaded into buying any add-on extras at this stage.
- Try to find just one friend already hooked and seek his advice.
- Check that there is on-site (ie at your home) service for at least one year.
- Don't read too many computer magazines; it will only confuse you.

IT'S A COMPUTER WORLD

- Decide if you want colour printing or not and see a sample of any printer's output before you buy.
- Don't buy additional manuals (even 'idiot'-type guides) for your particular software before you have used your computer for a while and have grasped the basics. Then list a few queries you have and compare manuals to see which one answers them and in the least confusing manner.
- Buy the highest graded technology you can afford at the time.

Happy computing!

9 TAKING A BREAK - OR TWO!

- Holidays, holidays...
- Especially for singles
- For those with a handicap
- Health and insurance
- Securing your home

Life won't be quite one long holiday now that you have retired, but you can approach that ideal with careful planning - and of course sufficient money in the bank. Even then holidays are unlikely to cost you as much as they did before, for two reasons: (a) you will not be restricted to peak periods, and (b) you are now one of a large army particularly attractive to holiday companies, who will go out of their way to sell you one of their special schemes.

At long last you may have moved up to the top of the 'holiday list', instead of having to wait for colleagues to choose first. No longer should you have to worry about school holidays, and those dreadful weekends when everyone appears to be on the move. Even getting there - avoiding crowds and taking advantage of concessionary tariffs - is going to be more enjoyable. This is, perhaps above all, one of the real joys of retirement.

TAKING A BREAK - OR TWO!

Holidays, Holidays . . .

All kinds of holidays are open to you, including a few that you might not have tried so far. Have you considered an activity holiday, or one that specialises in your favourite hobby or interest? Or a cruise, if these are new to you? Or visiting a health spa? Or even swapping your house for two weeks for one on the Florida coast? And if life is still a little pressured, what about going on a retreat where you can buy peace and quiet for a week or two?

The openings are limitless, and the most difficult decision may well be: What shall we try first? Below is just a small selection, categorised to give you a feel of the marketplace. Away you go!

Special offers

As already suggested, you are now a very attractive potential customer to the many holiday companies operating in the UK, and are likely to benefit with some of them from the age of 55. These holidays usually avoid the periods when schools are out, but they also make use of those hotels catering for the more selective client, ie you. So there are unlikely to be a hundred steps to the beach, dozens of night clubs in the vicinity or a five-mile trek to the nearest restaurant.

And talking of restaurants, you are likely to find like-minded folk in these; and (sometimes!) staff who understand the needs of a slightly older population.

MAKE THE MOST OF YOUR RETIREMENT

Saga Holidays is probably the leader in this field, and is well known for its speciality holidays for those whose tastes are a little more developed. Both Great Britain and overseas are covered. Thomson, Portland, First Choice (Leisurely Days), Co-operative Travel Care (Club 50+ Friends) and Cosmos (Golden Times) all have divisions which seek out resorts likely to be of special interest to pensioners, often where followers of dancing, bowling and similar pastimes can indulge themselves, sometimes day and night if they wish.

Hundreds of coach firms operate in the 'golden oldie' market, and British Rail runs Golden Rail Holidays especially for those seeking something a little quieter. Even Butlins and Pontins would like you to fill their places during off-peak periods, and they organise their entertainment accordingly. Pop into your travel agent to find out what is on offer.

If you are prepared to put up with fairly small bedrooms in order to save money, consider the many colleges and universities which find themselves with empty accommodation out of term. Either self-catering or bed and breakfast is usually available at modest rates, and families are catered for if you would like to take your grandchildren along with you! It is a convenient way of exploring interesting and historical cities such as York, Chester, Nottingham etc. Write to the British Universities Accommodation Consortium, Connect or, in Scotland, CampusHotels.

TAKING A BREAK - OR TWO!

If you are a caravanner (or still a camper) you will know of the Camping and Caravanning Club or the Caravan Club. The English Tourist Board can also put you in touch with a range of caravan parks across the country.

Look also for special magazine and newspaper offers. Choice magazine, for instance, can save you up to 10% all year round on holidays with Kuoni, Cosmos, British Airways, Thomson and others, providing they are booked through their agency.

Cultural trips

These can range from an archaeological visit to the Middle East, through guided tours of castles and stately homes of France and elsewhere, to a trip to the Edinburgh International Festival. You will obviously be influenced by your own special interests, and your local travel agent will be delighted to point the way.

Painting holidays in such places as Spain, Italy and Morocco are organised by Artscape, while Summer Music specialises in musical breaks all the year round. Ace Study Tours incorporates holidays with lessons on architecture, the history of art, archaeology, music, drama, ecology and wildlife. Voyages Jules Verne runs tours concentrating on natural history as well as painting. And so the list goes on.

Activity holidays

Hopefully you are still fit and active enough to take part in these - and once again, even if you have not experienced them before, do consider giving them a try. You will

MAKE THE MOST OF YOUR RETIREMENT

certainly find yourself in similar company if you are selective; many travel firms operate activity breaks aimed especially at the older end of the market.

One of the better known of these is the Ramblers' Association, which in conjunction with Ramblers Holidays Ltd organises walking tours that can be linked to special interests such as bird-spotting. Many of these are in places as far away as China and North America. If you prefer more up-market accommodation, but still like the walking (or cycling), the Alternative Travel Group Ltd. specialises in combining the two. They offer holidays in Britain or abroad, with groups kept small for intimacy, and often feature gourmet restaurants on their itinerary.

Countrywide Holidays base their holidaymakers at selected country houses, and walking is graded from easy to strenuous. Other activities, such as bridge, photography or folk dancing, are thrown in for good measure. Their Vintage Holidays scheme is worth looking at. English Wanderer offers holidays in a number of our famous and beautiful National Parks.

If you are really keen you could try the Sports Council for a free list of their coaching courses across the UK. Beginners are always welcome and those with a disability are sometimes catered for. The Scottish Sports Council has three centres offering courses at all skill levels. For golfers, Eurogolf runs breaks across mainland Europe and in America. If you would like to design your own golfing holiday, Great British Golf will give you a helping hand.

Cycling for Softies was established especially for those who like to take their cycling reasonably easy; participants pedal across France and cycles are included in the price. If

TAKING A BREAK - OR TWO!

you want to go at your own pace, Just Pedalling will fix up bed and breakfast accommodation for you - and lend you one of their bikes!

Fishermen are catered for through Anglers World Holidays which takes in all the best fishing spots in the world, with accommodation in local farmhouses, cottages and the like, organised on your behalf. Both fly/drive and sail/drive versions are offered.

Craft holidays

Following an interest in a specific art or craft while on holiday has never been easier. Hundreds of centres now arrange this, offering accommodation ranging from country mansions to student bedrooms, with prices differing accordingly.

These holidays cater to an amazing variety of interests. For instance, you can enjoy needlework classes set in Hampton Court Palace (The Royal School of Needlework), or pottery in Somerset (Millfield School Village of Education). You can practise weaving, spinning and dyeing in Wales (Martin and Nina Weatherhead); clock repairing and book binding in West Sussex (Old Rectory); and basketmaking in Essex (The Basketmakers' Association). Whatever craft you are interested in, there will be something to keep you busy on holiday. The Crafts Council will have a full list, and be able to tell you who runs what and where.

MAKE THE MOST OF YOUR RETIREMENT

Holidaying with wine

Taking in wine tastings while on holiday can only add to the pleasure and there are a number of tour companies now specialising in these. Obvious destinations include France, Portugal, Spain; but now less traditional wine-making areas can also be visited and sampled - California and Australia, for example.

Wine Journeys and World Wine Tours Ltd. both revel in taking holidaymakers who enjoy their wines around the vineyards of the world. Masters of Wine will normally accompany you, and numbers travelling together are kept quite small.

If you would like to make your own way around some of the many home-grown wine makers, write to the English Vineyards Association for a list of those throwing open their doors.

Beyond these suggestions, browse among travel brochures in any good agent's office, and ask them what they have available on the wine scene.

Retreats

You will be surprised, if you attend one of these, at just how popular they are with folk seeking nothing more than peace and quiet for a few days - even though they may already be retired! There are no less than 200 or so in the UK, and The National Retreat Association will let you have a list of these if you write to them.

TAKING A BREAK - OR TWO!

Some have religious associations such as Allington Castle (Carmelite), Pluscarden Abbey (Roman Catholic; men only) and Parcevall Hall (Anglican), but others are ecumenical (like The Iona Community) or, indeed, have no such connections - such as The Hen House Club, which caters solely for women of all denominations.

Being away from it all does not mean you are completely cut off from society. Expect to meet people of similar minds who will be delighted to converse with you. What will be absent will be the more active and sometimes noisier side of a traditionally 'standard' holiday.

Cruising

You don't need to be retired to cruise, but this type of holiday has always tended to attract an older clientele. On the other hand it is one of the fastest growing types of holiday, and you are likely to see a number of younger adult faces on board these days, some of them with children.

For those who have yet to try a cruise, it is probably the most relaxing way to spend your money and at the same time receive real value for it. Initially some cruise prices (but only some - you can cruise abroad from around £500) appear very expensive. But remember that once on board, particularly on those cruises not visiting ports, the only additional expenditure you can incur is on drinks - and perhaps an item or two from the ship's limited goods shop. On a more normal holiday, as you will know, you are constantly putting your hand in your pocket for taxis, meals out, ice-creams and the like.

None of that for the cruise passenger. Prices quoted are fully inclusive, apart perhaps from any airport taxes, and gratuities - although many ships now incorporate on-board gratuities in the price. So your payment includes everything you can possibly eat or drink (non-alcoholic) on an almost non-stop basis! The larger liners boast several restaurants and cafes, and there is usually at least one of these open for up to 18 hours a day. Midnight feasts, at which magnificent ice statues and other culinary delights await delighted guests, are now commonplace.

There is hardly a spot in the world where you cannot cruise. Trips range from cross-Atlantic voyages to more sedate meanders along the Nile or the Mississippi. Round-the-world cruises cost a lot more, but don't try one of these until you have convinced yourself that ship life is for you. Although my hunch is it will be.

P & O Cruises and Princess Cruises are two of the leaders in this field and will almost certainly guarantee not to disappoint you. But there are several others, and another trip to the travel agents is called for!

Home exchanges

Exchanging your house - and possibly car and family pet - for a spell at a complete stranger's home may not be everyone's idea of a holiday, but hundreds do it enjoyably every year, and recommend it to others. Unless you already have friends who are equally keen on the idea, you are better off with a recognised swapping agency. There are several, including:

TAKING A BREAK - OR TWO!

- World-wide Home Exchange Club, which covers 35 countries and has some 1,500 customers. You don't have to offer up your own home and can merely take advantage of those on offer.
- Entente Cordiale Bureau specialising in North America and France.
- Home Base Holidays. This company will list your home for you and circulate details of it to its other members, but final arrangements then rest with you.
- Intervac International Home Exchange covers more than 50 countries and claims to have almost 10,000 customers.

All of these companies will provide you with advice on such practicalities as the kind of instructions to leave your guests, and the legal position should anything go wrong. Providing the introduction is respectably based it is unlikely that anything major should go wrong. More probably, both families will have the times of their lives and wish they had thought of it before! You will only have to find your return fare and, of course, living costs, but your accommodation will be free if you are operating a two-way swap. There is an annual registration fee for this kind of introduction ranging from £35 to £55.

Timesharing

This is examined briefly here, but you are strongly advised to take specialised legal advice (ie from a solicitor well versed in the timeshare market; try the Law Society if necessary) before you sign anything or pay over any money. Tales of holidaymakers persuaded to put down substantial deposits whilst on holiday, particularly in Spain and Portugal, are legion; don't allow the local sunshine to affect your judgement in this way. Seek advice also from The Timeshare Council.

Timesharing is quite straightforward. You pay over a sum of money on a once-only basis and that entitles you to stay in the property for, typically, one or two weeks each year for ever. And that really is for ever - when you die, you can transfer ownership to a relative or friend. There are, however, some continuing costs such as maintenance and repairs, decoration or perhaps a regular maid service, and all of these will be consolidated into a 'management charge' which can rise year by year. Your true cost therefore remains a constant unknown.

The initial lump sum payable can vary from around £2,000 to ten times this amount, depending upon the period in the year you select. You can elect to send friends or relations in place of yourself, although you will ultimately remain responsible for any damage caused.

Two well-known timeshare companies are Interval International Ltd. and RCI Ltd.

If you already own a timeshare but would like a change, exchanges (both temporarily and permanently) are sometimes available; but beware of unscrupulous companies offering to sell it for you. And again, seek advice from The Timeshare Council.

Shared *ownership* of a property, either abroad or at home, is a different matter. Legal advice is still essential. It can operate harmoniously, but equally it can become somewhat fraught if friends fall out. A tight legal agreement

TAKING A BREAK - OR TWO!

is a useful starting-point just in case. You (or your beneficiaries) may find it difficult to recoup your investment, and this should be borne in mind when making this kind of decision.

Several developers abroad can guide you along the legal footpath, including David Scott International and Trafalgar House Europe Resorts Ltd.

Learning a language

This subject is just as appropriate here as it would be in Chapter 6 (Finding Fresh Interests) because of the way in which you can enhance your holidays with a little proficiency in the local language. We are, as is well known, somewhat spoiled around the world since English is truly an international language and there is no real call upon us to learn another. Many of us have also been put off doing so because of the teaching methods we recall from schooldays. Forget these - today, learning a language can be fun.

With videos, cassettes and a host of initiatives developed by the major language tuition schools, the learning process becomes interactive (yes - you get to play a part!) and results can be quite spectacular. For around £100 or so - and a great deal of dedication - you will be amazed at what you are able to learn. Two mail-order companies specialising in European tongues are Accelerated Learning Systems Ltd. and BBC World-wide Ltd. For more concentrated and specific tuition, try one of the language schools such as the Italian Institute, the Goethe Institute

(German), or the Spanish Institute. Eurocentres or Universal Languages deal in most of the more popular foreign languages.

Learn where they speak the language

You can even combine increasing your language skills with the benefits of a foreign holiday through learning on location. Several institutions now offer residential learning courses in most of the major European languages including Russian. EF International Language Schools run courses from two to twelve weeks in places as exciting as Paris, Rome, Moscow, Beijing and even Costa Rica. Euro Language Services offer similar experience including special Third Age programmes for those aged from 50 to 70-plus.

Extra-curricular activities are tacked on and may include cookery classes along with visits to the local fruit and vegetable markets, botanical gardens and so on. Costs are reasonable and can include university style accommodation or staying with host families, which gives you extra practice in learning the language of your choice.

Especially For Singles

There's plenty out there for you as well. No longer does every holiday company automatically expect people to travel in pairs, and a number of companies now exist

TAKING A BREAK - OR TWO!

which cater purely for the sole traveller. Even the extra supplement for single rooms is beginning to disappear from some brochures.

Just a few of the specialists are:

- Saga Holidays Ltd. runs 'Specially for Singles' holidays, with couriers who keep a careful eye on everyone to make certain no-one's left out.
- Solo's Holidays Ltd. which cater exclusively for single men and women.
- Odyssey International whose holiday clients are aged up to 80.
- Travel Companions (UK) Ltd. if you are actively seeking someone to accompany you on holiday.

For Those With A Handicap

Access for those travelling by wheelchair, or who are a little frail on their legs, has improved significantly during recent years, following local and national government initiatives. More and more, lifts and ramps can be seen at airports, railway stations and other embarkation points. Both British Rail and the airlines issue booklets on what help is available.

The Holiday Care Service is a central source of information for those with special needs - physical or neurological - who are about to go on holiday. Bookings can be made on your behalf by the Service which will know of suitable hotels and apartments where accessibility is easier. No charge is made for this service. ATS Travel will make all the arrangements for you if you are disabled, including the provision of a door-to-door service if you wish.

Camping for the Disabled will find you a suitable campsite, while the Royal National Institute for the Blind has three specially fitted hotels by the sea. John Grooms Association for Disabled People can provide you with suitable flats, bungalows or caravans. Arthritis Care also operates its own holiday centres, and the Parkinson's Disease Society can advise on suitable locations for its sufferers.

Health And Insurance

You will obviously take advice from your doctor or pharmacist about staying healthy whilst on holiday. But also check on injections necessary for those out-of-the-way places you may now be visiting. Don't be put off by these; thousands of travellers are treated in this way every year and suffer no ill-effects. You tend to hear only of the few who experience a problem - and these are nearly always very temporary.

Modern medicines are available in most countries, with the exception of some spots in the Third World. But do go prepared with the basics, if only to save you the trouble of finding a chemist when you get there. Stomach upsets are more likely in places such as the Middle and Far East,

TAKING A BREAK - OR TWO!

Africa and South America. But if you follow sound advice such as not drinking the local water, your chances of staying fit and healthy will remain quite high.

Insurance is a must. You might consider an annual policy to save premiums if you foresee taking two or three holidays a year. Standard condition policies are now quite common and, providing you make use of one of the major companies, you don't really need to read all the small print. The Association of British Insurers will let you have details of the kinds of things you should be looking out for both at home and abroad.

Saga Holidays provides useful discounts on both European and world-wide cover for its members.

If you are over 55, shop around for the best quote, as rates vary quite widely. Age Concern Insurance Services will guide you.

Securing Your Home

If you are going to be away from home for longer than usual, or frequently, it will pay you to take a few moments to review your level of home security. Check, for instance, whether your insurance policy is still valid if you spend more than a certain number of days away; thirty is often a maximum allowed at any one time.

MAKE THE MOST OF YOUR RETIREMENT

If you don't have a Neighbourhood Watch scheme in your road, consider starting one now - they're extremely simple to run, very discreet and have cut crime in many areas. Speak to your local police.

Draw up a checklist for when you go on holiday. Apart from the obvious items, it should include:

- Asking neighbours to keep an eye on your property, including pushing any free newspapers or post through your letterbox.
- Leaving a telephone number where you or a relative can be contacted.
- Removing valuables from the house.
- Not leaving a key in an obvious spot such as under a doormat or flowerpot.
- Locking ladders securely.

ARP O50 offers discounts of at least 15% on house insurance to its members; membership is free if you take out one of its policies.

Hire a sitter

If you want to feel really safe, consider using one of the homesitting agencies now available; some also handle pets. The five majors are: Homesitters; Universal Aunts; Housewatch; Home and Pet Care; and Animal Aunts. If you live in or near Buckinghamshire there is the Featherbed Community Club for Dogs, which allows your pet to run free in two enclosed acres of parkland.

TAKING A BREAK - OR TWO!

These services are not cheap, but they do give you peace of mind. Sitters usually pay for their own food and travelling expenses. They will guarantee not to leave your home for more than about three hours a day, and they stay in all night.

Make certain you are happy with any local concerns offering a similar service before you commission them. The better companies will 'interview' you before taking you on.

10 LOOKING BACK - AND LOOKING AHEAD

- Keeping records
- Family trees
- Making a will
- Gifts to others
- Dealing with funerals
- New projects
- Repartnering
- Getting help in difficult times
- And finally . . .

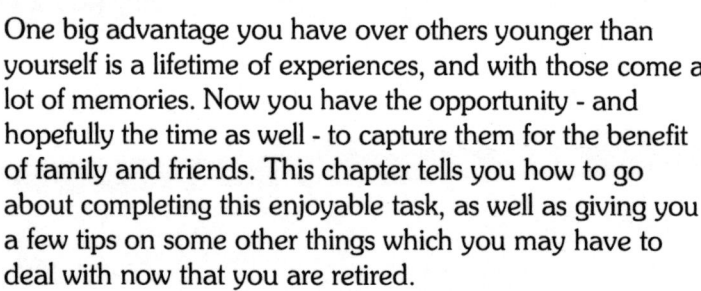

One big advantage you have over others younger than yourself is a lifetime of experiences, and with those come a lot of memories. Now you have the opportunity - and hopefully the time as well - to capture them for the benefit of family and friends. This chapter tells you how to go about completing this enjoyable task, as well as giving you a few tips on some other things which you may have to deal with now that you are retired.

If you haven't done so already for instance, you should make a will and at the same time ensure any liability to inheritance tax is minimal. You may want to consider donating organs for the benefit of others after your death. And the likelihood of having to arrange someone else's funeral, however sad this thought may be, cannot be

LOOKING BACK - AND LOOKING AHEAD

overlooked. On the other hand you may of course wish to make arrangements for your own departure, however far off it may be.

Now is also a golden opportunity to do something special you have always wanted to do but never had the time to start (or complete), and we consider this under New Projects.

For those of you who are single, whether by choice or through death or separation, there is still the option to seek a partner, and we take a look at the best way to go about this delicate assignment.

Some organisations you might like to have a note of in case of need are also listed.

Keeping Records

You don't have to be a writer, nor do you need to launch yourself into a full-length book (unless you really want to!), but your next of kin will appreciate your noting down certain notable events in your life to make sure these are not forgotten when family histories are being retold in the future. Grandchildren, in particular, love to hear what Granddad and Grandma did when they were their age on their holidays, or when and where they got married. It would be a pity if all this were lost in the mists of time.

To help you put things in order there are some very attractive books available such as 'Grandmother's Album' in which can be stored memories of your own grandparents along with details of when you were small, from schooldays through growing up, to meeting your partner and finally starting your own family. There's space for photographs and other mementoes, as well as spots in which you can recall particularly favourite memories.

This is by far the easiest way of marshalling all this information and the books are not over-expensive. Alternatively you can make your own, especially if you are artistic, and this would give it a personal touch.

Details fascinate

Put in the little things as well as the big. Memories of the price of sweets, or how you came to first meet your partner are all fascinating details for those who know you well. They are snippets that will be treasured for ever.

Remember also to record details on the reverse of family photographs. There is nothing more frustrating than finding a picture of Granny when young, with a couple of admirers, and not knowing who they were! Just names and dates will do; make this one of your first projects.

The Mass Observation Archive was established in the 1930's, using 2,000 voluntary observers to study everyday life in Britain. Today there are only a quarter of that number and more are needed.

LOOKING BACK - AND LOOKING AHEAD

Speak your mind

The Oral History Society has been set up to support and advise people interested in recording personal histories. It also runs regular workshops and conferences to encourage the filling in of gaps that would otherwise emerge in the history of our families. Individual membership is quite cheap.

Family Trees

You could spend the rest of your lifetime tracing your ancestors and, although two or three generations usually suffice, it is likely that if you get that far you won't want to stop!

The drawing up of family trees is big business today and you will probably find genealogical courses are held at your local college. There are residential courses and holiday breaks that specialise in this fascinating subject, as well as the help offered by The Society of Genealogists who will send you a quarterly magazine if you join, and provide access to their large library.

Providing your family tree stretches back within the United Kingdom, then church and parish records will send you off on all sorts of remarkable trails and you may well find yourself captivated by the subject. There is also a wide selection of books available on genealogy. Computer buffs can buy an appropriate program.

Foreign connections may be more difficult (and expensive) to track down but they will certainly be more fun and could lead you to new holiday venues never before contemplated. A number of local societies exist which always welcome new members.

Making A Will

This you must do if you have not already done so. A remarkable one in three of us fails to pass on a note of our wishes (that is all a will is, after all), leaving our next of kin to sort out our affairs, usually at great cost and quite frequently involving arguments which could easily have been avoided.

Why you should do it

If you die without leaving a will, the State will step in and apply its own rules -and they may not be particularly favourable either to your estate or to your dependants. Your partner, for instance, will not necessarily inherit all your estate and some of it may have to be sold to pay off other beneficiaries. If you have made a will but have since remarried, then the old will is automatically revoked in the eyes of the law and will not count for anything; you must make a new one.

If you are not married to your partner, he or she has no basic legal rights to your estate following your death and this may conflict with your intentions. The right to a previous spouse's estate is also lost if you are divorced.

LOOKING BACK - AND LOOKING AHEAD

Worse still, the taxman may take a bigger cut if you have not made a will in which you have taken legal advantage of our intestacy laws. More details are provided in Chapter 2 under Inheritance Tax.

Use a solicitor

Making a will is straightforward once you have given some thought to your wishes. A solicitor will translate these into the legal language necessary, and a home-made will is not advised. It could cause a hundredfold more trouble than you might have saved in the first place; the charge for drawing up two separate wills is quite modest. There are a few technicalities to adhere to but your solicitor will advise you on these; beneficiaries, for example, cannot include witnesses or their spouses.

Do not feel that, because you are about to make a will, you are going to die, although it is this fallacy which prevents many people from following such a course. You wouldn't dream of leaving to catch a train without making the necessary arrangements, ie finding out what time it runs and how much the journey will cost. Don't, therefore, go into the next world without having tidied up your affairs here first.

Contact the Law Society if you are not familiar with solicitors. Legal aid is available to certain people to help them with the cost of drawing up a will. The Society also produces a Personal Assets Log which provides your next of kin with details of your solicitor and where important items, such as your will, life policies and so on, can be found.

Keep it simple

Keep your wishes as simple as possible. There is no need to detail every possession and its ultimate beneficiary, but you might care to list special items and request your executors (those appointed to administer your will) to see that your wishes are followed. Solicitors usually offer an executor service, but a specialist is recommended: for example a bank's Executor and Trustee department or a larger firm of solicitors which employs a partner or manager to look solely after the administration of wills. Your original will can then be left with them, with a copy retained by yourself. You may need to update your will every five years or so depending upon any changes in your circumstances.

The law in Northern Ireland relating to wills is similar to that operating in England but Scotland has its own rules. Your solicitor will soon put you right.

Gifts To Others

You can reduce the amount of your inheritance tax liability by making regular gifts to family or friends. The law allows you to give away cash or gifts to the value of £3,000 each year as well as numerous small gifts of no more than £250. These are not included when it comes to assessing your after-death tax bill.

Any other gifts however, made in the period seven years before your death, will be counted, or part counted, before the 40% tax liability is calculated. If you are contemplating

LOOKING BACK - AND LOOKING AHEAD

making such gifts, speak to your accountant or a solicitor before doing so. It is essential, for instance, that the gift is made 'without reservation', ie that the donor gives up all rights and interests in it. You cannot 'give' away your house to your children - in the eyes of the tax authorities - and still live in it.

Helping charities

Deeds of covenant, under which you pledge money for a minimum of three years, are really only useful for charitable donations; the Charities Aid Foundation will gladly help you with the paperwork. You are not advised to draw up a Deed of Covenant yourself. You can also give to charity through the government's Give As You Earn scheme even though you are drawing a pension. Providing you are paying tax, your donations will avoid this, and all large charities have the necessary forms for you to complete.

Gift Aid is another method of helping your favourite charity if you are prepared to give at least £250 a time. All these government schemes are detailed in Inland Revenue leaflet IR65.

Your will can incorporate gifts to charity (legacies) and, indeed, charities benefit annually by about £1bn by this method. If worded carefully, your beneficiaries will avoid paying inheritance tax on legacies; but make sure you know the charity's precise requirements, and use a solicitor.

Helping others afterwards

'Life - don't keep it to yourself' is the well-known slogan of the NHS Organ Donor Register, with which thousands of people have registered in order to help others after their death. Anyone can become a donor; to signify your willingness ask at your doctor's surgery, or write to the Register for a free donor card, which is best carried at all times.

The major donor organs are the kidneys, heart, lungs, liver and pancreas as well as heart valves, other muscular tissue and the cornea. This last, the front part of the tough outer shell of the eyeball, enables others to see through your eyes.

Technically, if you have registered, your organs may be used for transplantation without consulting anyone else, in practice doctors will not remove organs if any of your relatives objects. The body is treated with complete respect, and organs are removed in the same way as with a live patient. Funerals are not delayed by the process.

Although strict confidentiality is maintained, your relatives will normally be told how your organ donation was used and the outcome of the transplant operations. Most are highly successful, and in this way some of the relatives' grief can be assuaged.

Dealing With Funerals

Apart from making a will there are other plans you and your partner can make if you wish.

LOOKING BACK - AND LOOKING AHEAD

Many people are concerned about funeral costs, which on average may amount to over £1,500. A policy can be taken out on your own or your partner's life for a fixed sum which can go a long way towards meeting this bill.

Alternatively, and gaining popularity over here after being introduced some years ago in America, is the pre-paid funeral plan which ensures all costs are covered and your personal wishes met. Any funeral parlour will provide you with details, although Dignity Ltd, Age Concern, Golden Charter and the Co-operative Society all run these schemes on a national basis. You pay today's prices and are then guaranteed a funeral to an agreed standard no matter how much longer you live.

Smaller funeral companies have also banded together to provide a similar scheme, though usually with greater flexibility of choice, through their national body the National Association of Funeral Directors. Either a lump sum or monthly contributions can be pre-paid.

If you are concerned about the state of a relative's grave that is some distance away, contact Pilgrim Services who will tidy it up for you for a fee. They will also send you 'before' and 'after' photographs.

If you have to deal with the death of a pet, or wish to plan ahead, Pet Funeral Services will provide you with a complete service involving either burial or cremation. They can handle anything from a canary to a pony.

New Projects

As well as having more time to follow existing interests, you now have the time to delve into something completely new and exciting.

It could be anything at all within your physical and financial capabilities, and for some this has included climbing Everest, 'adopting' a new family or spending a year or two on an overseas project. It could be a 'one-off' item or something which becomes a part of your new life for many years to come.

If you are still fit and active, take some moments out to consider - with your partner if you have one - exactly what might reinvigorate your life and, in a different kind of way, take the place of the working environment to which you have become accustomed.

Keep your brain active

Consider visiting a country you have never been to before (it need not be on the other side of the world - Ireland has many attractions!), taking up a completely new hobby (what about video making or fishing?), learning a new skill (carpentry or cross-stitch?) or joining a club which holds regular social events. It doesn't matter what it is; the objective is to get your brain cells working on something they are not used to, and provide you with an interest that you can completely immerse yourself in whenever you feel like it.

As much as anything it is the contrast that is important, and you should aim at something that is largely different from anything you have ever known. It needs to attract your genuine interest, of course; you should not allow yourself to be talked into a project that has no appeal.

It is sensible to approach it slowly and deliberately rather than committing yourself to something fully on day one. Features may emerge which you had not considered earlier and you should not be ashamed of dropping an idea if it doesn't turn out to be quite what you expected. There's a whole new range out there to experiment with.

Repartnering

If you are on your own when you reach retirement, whether by choice or otherwise, you should not write off the possibility of taking up the rest of your life with someone else if this is what you would really prefer.

It isn't easy to find a new partner at this stage in your life but then, if you recall, you probably had to work at it when you were a lot younger! Take heart in the extra experience and maturity you can now boast which should at least make choosing a new partner more of a science than the art it used to be.

MAKE THE MOST OF YOUR RETIREMENT

Meet more people

It will naturally be more difficult for the shy, retiring type than the extrovert, and only you can make adjustments to your own nature. The more people you mix with, the more likely you are to find a suitable partner. It is as scientific as that, so if your current circle is a restricted one then consider, firstly, ways of increasing it. Are you a member of clubs or societies that follow your interests? Do you participate in coach outings or group holidays? And then, of course, there are the clearly defined singles organisations - including ones especially for the over-55s.

Personal ads

If all this is beyond you, consider replying to some of the hundreds of advertisements for partners which appear in the 'personal' columns of so many magazines and newspapers these days. They go under a variety of names, from 'Saturday Rendezvous' in The Times to 'Eyelove' in Private Eye. Provided you take obvious security precautions and meet, at least the first time, in a public place, this can be a fun way to search for a mate - although don't expect to find the perfect person right away! A more sedate version of the personals is the Companion Network Directory, run by the Association of Retired Persons, to which you can subscribe.

Introduction or dating agencies

You may feel more at ease using a private introduction or dating agency. The agency will charge you a fee for its services, of course; and as with personal ads, you need to

LOOKING BACK - AND LOOKING AHEAD

have realistic expectations. But it's worth a try - you could become one of the many thousands of satisfied clients who have found partners this way.

There are hundreds of agencies operating in the UK. Many advertise in the 'personal ads' section of newspapers and magazines, and the Association of British Introduction Agencies can provide you with a list of their members. I have listed a few representative agencies in the Help List: look out for Two's Company, Dateplan and Mature Friends.

Anyone can register with an agency, just as anyone can take out or reply to a personal ad, so again, never meet for the first time anywhere other than in a public place. Blind dating is far from easy, and most people approach it with trepidation. If these are your feelings, you can be assured that you will not be alone. Despite this, every year, thousands of couples who first meet on a blind date bond together successfully.

If a relationship does look like becoming serious there can be items to resolve, such as where you should both set up home. True love can usually overcome all, and you shouldn't allow these concerns to overshadow what might become a very satisfying new chapter in your life.

Getting Help In Difficult Times

Throughout this book you will find names of organisations offering specialised help across a wide spectrum of activities. But the kind of help you may need could be more general. It could relate, for instance, to coping with bereavement, handling financial affairs, or the thousand and one other challenges which arise from time to time.

It's good to talk

Merely talking through a problem with someone with a sympathetic ear can be sufficient to bring relief, as many with a kindly doctor will testify. Bottling up a difficulty will only make it - and probably you - worse. So make your first port of call someone in whom you have trust and who is prepared to listen. If this isn't a family member it might well be a neighbour, close friend, doctor or the lady at the social services office. It doesn't matter who it is as long as you feel you can open up your heart to them and, at the same time, trust in them implicitly.

Resolving problems in this communicative way is an age-old practice. Try it first of all, and if it does fail, seek out a specialist.

Specialist help

This, again, could be your family doctor, nurse or social worker, but it could also be someone at your local Citizens' Advice Bureau, for instance. This should be listed in your telephone directory; if not, refer to their National Association address in the Help List at the end of this book. CAB volunteers are trained to have a sympathetic ear, and they can add to this a wealth of experience and knowledge on almost any subject you bring to their attention.

LOOKING BACK - AND LOOKING AHEAD

Specialists in dealing with those who have been recently bereaved include the National Association of Bereavement Services, who will put you in touch with a local office; the National Association of Widows which has branches throughout the UK; and CRUSE with its 200 branches. All are there to provide positive help. Don't attempt to mourn on your own if it is affecting your health.

For those with armed forces associations, there exist the War Widows Association of Great Britain and the Forces Help Society. If you contact either of these bodies you will find yourself in the company of others in similar circumstances, who are thus able to offer appropriate solace and comfort.

Other help sources include Counsel and Care for the Elderly, the British Association for Counselling, which holds a central register, and, in Northern Ireland, the Northern Ireland Association for Counselling. Those of Jewish faith may care to contact the Central Council for Jewish Community Services.

And Finally....

Now that you have joined the ranks of 'older people' - at least in the eyes of others! - you will have to learn to bear the brunt of a few hoary old misconceptions attaching themselves to this section of the populace.

Traditionally, the elderly are seen as irritable, bored, lonely, poor, frail and even senile. In practice you and I know that most of these adjectives are unrecognisable.

MAKE THE MOST OF YOUR RETIREMENT

This has been confirmed by a survey carried out by the American Association of Retired Persons of their over 33 million members.

The majority of these have confirmed:

- their ongoing good health;
- renewed interest in a thousand and more hobbies and pastimes;
- participation in social activities at a higher level than before;
- satisfactory levels of income; and
- continued sexual activity.

What more could you ask for?

So congratulate yourself on becoming another member of a growing band of 'new men and women', eager to explore new avenues, reach extended heights and - quite frequently - beginning to enjoy themselves more than ever before.

Don't waste any time in signing up for such a fabulous club!

HELP LIST

Chapter 1: Getting Yourself Unorganised

ACTIVE LIFE
Aspen Specialist Media PLC, Christ Church, Cosway Street, London NW1 5NJ.
TEL 0171-262-2622

ASSOCIATION OF BRITISH INSURERS
51 Gresham Street, London EC2V 7HQ.
Tel 0171-600-3333

ASSOCIATION OF RETIRED PERSONS
3rd Floor, Greencoat House, Francis Street, London SW1P 1DZ.
Tel 0171-828-0500

CHOICE MAGAZINE
Apex House, Oundle Road, Peterborough PE2 9NP.
Tel 01733-555123

DRAUGHT PROOFING ADVISORY ASSOCIATION
PO Box 12, Haslemere, Surrey GU27 3AH.
Tel 01428-654011

FINANCIAL TIMES
1 Southward Bridge, London, SE1 9HL.
Tel 0171-873-3000

THE GLASS AND GLAZING FEDERATION
44-48 Borough High Street, London SE1 1XB.
Tel 0171-403-7177

LEASEHOLD ENFRANCHISEMENT ADVISORY SERVICE
6-8 Maddox Street, London W1R 9PN.
Tel 0171-493-3116

NATIONAL ASSOCIATION OF LOFT INSULATION CONTRACTORS
PO Box 12, Haslemere, Surrey GU27 3AH.
Tel 01428-654011

OPEN UNIVERSITY
PO Box 200, Walton Hall, Milton Keynes MK7 6YZ.
Tel 01908-653231

MAKE THE MOST OF YOUR RETIREMENT

PRE-RETIREMENT ASSOCIATION OF GREAT BRITAIN AND NORTHERN IRELAND
26 Frederick Sanger Rd., Surrey Research Park, Guildford, Surrey, GU2 5YD.
Tel 01483-301170

THE RETIREMENT TRUST
19 Borough High Street, London Bridge, London SE1 9SE.
Tel 0171-378-9708

SAGA HOLIDAYS LTD. (& SAGA MAGAZINE CLUB)
Saga Building, Freepost, Folkestone, Kent CT20 1BR.
Tel 0800-300500 (Reservations); 0800-300456 (Brochures)

SCOTTISH PRE-RETIREMENT COUNCIL
Alexandra House, 204 Bath Street, Glasgow G2 4HL.
Tel 0141-332-9427

UNIVERSITY OF THE THIRD AGE
National Office, 1 Stockwell Green, London SW9 9JF.
Tel 0171-737-2541

WORKERS EDUCATIONAL ASSOCIATION
Temple House, 17 Victoria Park Square, Bethnal Green, London E2 9PB.
Tel 0181-983-1515

WORLD OF RETIREMENT
7 Dingle Ave., Denton, Manchester, M34 7RB.
Tel 0161-320-0149

YOURS MAGAZINE
Apex House, Oundle Road, Peterborough PE2 9NP.
Tel 01733-555123

Chapter 2: Recalculating Your Finances

ASSOCIATION OF POLICY MARKET MAKERS
Tel 0171-739-3949

BENEFITS AGENCY (DSS)
RPFA Unit, Room 37D, DSS Longbenton, Benton Park Road, Newcastle-upon-Tyne NE98 1YX

CONSUMERS ASSOCIATION
2 Marylebone Road, London NW1 4DX.
Tel 0171-486-5544

HELP LIST

DSS (OVERSEAS BRANCH)
Newcastle upon Tyne NE98 1YX.
Tel 0191-213-5000

FINANCIAL INTERMEDIARIES, MANAGERS AND BROKERS REGULATORY ASSOCIATION (FIMBRA).
Tel 0171-538-8860

INDEPENDENT FINANCIAL ADVISORS
Tel 01483-461461

LIFE ASSURANCE AND UNIT TRUST REGULATORY ORGANISATION (LAUTRO)
Tel 0171-379-0444

LONDON STOCK EXCHANGE
Old Broad Street, London EC2N 1HP.
Tel 0171-797-1000

MONEY FACTS
Money Publications, Laundry Loke, North Walsham, Norfolk NR28 0BD.
Tel 01692-500765 (£48.50 per annum)

OCCUPATIONAL PENSIONS ADVISORY SERVICE
11 Belgrave Road, London SW1V 1RB.
Tel 0171-233-8080

Chapter 3: Family And Friends

AID-CALL
Linhay, Ashburton, Devon TQ13 7UP.
Tel 01364-654321

ASSOCIATION OF BRITISH INTRODUCTION AGENCIES
23 Abingdon Road, London LW8 6AL.
Tel 0171-938-1011

ASSOCIATION OF RETIRED PERSONS
3rd Floor, Greencoat House, Francis Street, London SW1P 1DZ.
Tel 0171-828-0500

CANUSPA
Mrs. Pat Roome, 77 King John Avenue, King's Lynn.

CARE AND REPAIR LTD
Castle House, Kirtley Drive, Nottingham NG7 1LD.
Tel 0115-9799091;
Fax 0115-9859457

MAKE THE MOST OF YOUR RETIREMENT

CHILDREN NEED GRANDPARENTS
2 Surrey Way, Laindon, West Basildon, Essex SS15 6PS. (Enclose sae)

DISABILITY ACTION
2 Annadale Avenue, Belfast BT7 3JR.
Tel 01232-491011

DISABILITY SCOTLAND
Princes House, 5 Shandwick Place, Edinburgh EH2 4RG.
Tel 0131-229-8632

FRIENDS BY POST
43 Chatsworth Road, High Lane, Stockport, Cheshire SK6 8DA (Send sae)

LOST TOUCH
Teletext Ltd., PO Box 297, London SW6 1XT

NATIONAL ASSOCIATION OF WIDOWS PEN CLUB
9 Boston Close, Springdale Park, Darlington, Co. Durham DL1 2RF

NATIONAL COUNCIL FOR ONE PARENT FAMILIES
255 Kentish Town Road, London NW5 2LX. (Send large sae for details)

NATIONAL PENSIONERS CONVENTION
4 Stevens Street, Lowestoft, Suffolk NR32 2JE.
Tel 01502-565807

ROYAL ASSOCIATION FOR DISABILITY AND REHABILITATION (RADAR)
12 City Forum, 250 City Road, London EC1V 8AF.
Tel 0171-250-3222

ROYAL BRITISH LEGION
Aylesford, Kent ME20 7NX.
Tel 01622-717172

SOLITAIRE
PO Box 2, Hockley, Essex SS5 4QR (Send sae)
TOC H, 1 Forest Close, Wendover, Bucks. HP22 6BT.
Tel 01296-623911

WALES COUNCIL FOR THE DISABLED
Llys Ifor, Crescent Road, Caerphilly, Mid-Glamorgan CF8 1XL.
Tel 01222-887325

HELP LIST

Chapter 4: Looking After Your Health

ARTHRITIS CARE
18 Stephenson Way, London NW1 2HD.
Tel 0171-916-1500

THE ASSOCIATION OF SEXUAL AND MARITAL THERAPISTS
P.O. Box 62, Sheffield, S10 3TS

VERA BADLEY
c/o Cluett Burns, Unit 6, Solent Industrial Estate, Hedge End, Southampton, SO30 2FX

BMI
Dacre House, 19 Dacre Street, London SW1H 0DH.
Tel 0171-222-1202;
Fax. 0171-222-0373

BUPA
see local telephone directory or ring 0800-800455 (freephone)

BRITISH DEAF ASSOCIATION
1-3 Worship Street, London EC2A 2AB.
Tel 0171-588-3520

BRITISH HEALTH CARE ASSOCIATION
24a Main Street, Garforth, Leeds LS25 1AA.
Tel 0113-2320903

BRITISH HEART FOUNDATION
Freepost, Bristol, BS38 7AX

BRITISH TINNITUS ASSOCIATION
Room 6, 14-18 West Bar Green, Sheffield S1 2DA.
Tel 0114-2796600

MARRIAGE COUNSELLING SCOTLAND
105 Hanover Square, Edinburgh EH2 1DJ.
Tel 0131-225-5006

NATIONAL BACK PAIN ASSOCIATION
16 Elmtree Road, Teddington, Middlesex TW11 8ST.
Tel 0181-977-5474

NUFFIELD HOSPITALS
PO Box 420, Southampton SO17 2XJ.
Tel 01703-582004

PPP HEALTHCARE
Freepost WC 1244, Stratford upon Avon, CV37 6BR.
Tel 0800-585059

MAKE THE MOST OF YOUR RETIREMENT

PHOBIC ACTION
Claybury Grounds, Manor Road, Woodford Green, Essex IG8 8PR.
Tel 0181-559-2551

THE PHOBICS SOCIETY
4 Cheltenham Road, Chorlton-cum-Hardy, Manchester M21 1QN.
Tel 0161-881-1937
QUITLINE Tel 0800-002200

RELATE
Herbert Gray College, Little Church Street, Rugby CV21 3AP.
Tel 01788-573241

RESEARCH INTO AGEING
15-17 St. Cross Street, London EC1N 8UN.

ROYAL NATIONAL INSTITUTE FOR DEAF PEOPLE
19-23 Featherstone Street, London EC1Y 8SL.
Tel 0171-296-8000

SMOKELINE
0800-848484 (Noon to midnight; 7 days a week)

Chapter 5: Eat For Health

HEALTH EDUCATION AUTHORITY
Hamilton House, Mabledon Place, London WC1H 9TX.
Tel 0171-383-3833

SOIL ASSOCIATION
86 Colston Street, Bristol BS1 5BB

WEIGHT WATCHERS (UK) LTD.
Kidwells Park House, Kidwells Park Drive, Maidenhead, Berks. SL6 8YT.
Tel 01628-777077

WEIGHT WATCHERS BY MAIL
Freepost, North Shields, Tyne and Wear NE2 6BR.
Tel 0191-2962200

WOMEN'S NUTRITIONAL ADVISORY SERVICE
PO Box 268, Lewes, East Sussex BN7 2QN.
Tel 01273-487366

HELP LIST

Chapter 6: Finding Fresh Interests

AGATHA CHRISTIE SOCIETY
PO Box 985, London SW1X 9XA.

ALLISON AND BUSBY
179 King's Cross Road, London WC1X 9BZ.
Tel 0171-833-1042

ANTIQUE COLLECTORS CLUB
5 Church Street, Woodbridge, Suffolk IP12 1DS.
Tel 013943-5501

ARTS COUNCIL (England)
14 St. Peter Street, London SW1P 3NQ.
Tel 0171-333-0100 (in Scotland, 12 Manor Place, Edinburgh EH3 7DD. Tel 0131-226-6051; in Wales, Holst House, Museum Place, Cardiff CF1 3NX. Tel 01222-394711; in Northern Ireland, 181 Stranmillis Road, Belfast BT9 5DU. Tel 01232-381591)

AS TIME GOES BY
The Old Dairy, Charles Street, Droylsden, Manchester M43 6HD

BBC TICKET UNITS
(Radio) Broadcasting House, London W1A 1AA (Television) Wood Lane, Shepherds Bush, London W12 7RJ

BT
Tel 0800-800860 (for flexi-working; freephone)

A & C BLACK (PUBLISHERS) LTD.
35 Bedford Row, London WC1R 4JH.
Tel 0171-242-0946; Fax. 0171-831-8478

BIBLIOPHILE BOOKS
5 Thomas Road, London E14 7BN.
Tel 0171-515-9222

BRITISH ASSOCIATION OF NUMISMATIC SOCIETIES
Bush Boake Allen Ltd., Blackhouse Lane, London E17 5QP

MAKE THE MOST OF YOUR RETIREMENT

BRITISH COUNCIL OF BALLROOM DANCING
87 Parkhurst Road,
Holloway, London N7 0LP.
Tel 0171-609-1386

BRITISH FILM INSTITUTE
21 Stephen Street, London W1P 1PL.
Tel 0171-255-1444

BRITISH MODEL SOLDIER SOCIETY
22 Priory Gardens, Hampton, Middlesex TW12 2PZ.
Tel 0181-979-7137

BUSINESS MONEY FACTS
Laundry Loke, North Walsham, Norfolk NR28 0BD.
Tel 01692-500765;
Fax. 01692-500865

CINNAMON TRUST
Poldarves Farm, Trescowe Common, Germoe, Penzance TR20 9RX.
Tel 01736-850291

THE CIVIC TRUST
17 Carlton House Terrace, London SW1Y 5AW.
Tel 0171-930-0914

CORPS OF COMMISSIONAIRES
Market House, 85 Cowcross Street, London EC1M 6BP.
Tel 0171-490-1125

COUNCIL FOR THE ACCREDITATION OF CORRESPONDENCE COLLEGES
27 Marylebone Road, London NW1 5JS.
Tel 0171-935-5391

THE COUNTRYSIDE COMMISSION (England)
John Dower House, Crescent Place, Cheltenham GL50 2RA.
Tel 01242-521381;
in Scotland, Battleby, Redgorten, Perth PH1 3EW.
Tel 0131-4474784

CRAFTS COUNCIL
44a Pentonville Road, Islington, London N1 9BY.
Tel 0171-278-7700

ENGLISH FOLK DANCE AND SONG SOCIETY
Cecil Sharp House, 2 Regents Park Road, London NW1 7AY.
Tel 0171-485-2206

HELP LIST

FORESTRY COMMISSION
231 Corstorphine Road,
Edinburgh EH12 7AT.
Tel 0131-334-0303

THE GARDEN STUDIO
Cores End Cottage, Bourne
End, Bucks. SL8.
Tel 01628-524855

HANDBELL RINGERS OF GREAT BRITAIN
9 Dale Road, Grantham,
Lincs. NG31 8EF.
Tel 01476-591986

HORTICULTURAL THERAPY
Goulds Ground, Vallis Way,
Frome, Somerset BA11 3DW.
Tel 01373-464782

MERCURY COMMUNICATIONS
Tel 0500-500194 (Freephone re flexi-working)

MOTABILITY
Gate House, West Gate,
Harlow, Essex CM20 1HR.
Tel 01279-635666

NATIONAL ASSOCIATION OF DISABLEMENT INFORMATION AND ADVICE SERVICES
Park Lodge, St. Catherine's
Hospital, Tickhill Road, Balby,
Doncaster DN4 8QN.
Tel 01302-310123

NATIONAL EXTENSION COLLEGE
18 Brooklands Avenue,
Cambridge CB2 2HN.
Tel 01223-316644

NATIONAL GARDENS SCHEME
Hatchlands Park, East
Clandon, Guildford, Surrey
GU4 7RT.
Tel 01483-211535

NATIONAL PHILATELIC SOCIETY
107 Charterhouse Street,
London EC1M 6PT.
Tel 0171-251-5040

OPEN COLLEGE OF THE ARTS
Houndhill, Worsborough,
Barnsley, South Yorks. S70 6TU.
Tel 0891-168902

MAKE THE MOST OF YOUR RETIREMENT

OPEN UNIVERSITY
PO Box 724, Walton Hall,
Milton Keynes MK7 6ZS.
Tel 01908-653231

PET FOSTERING SERVICE SCOTLAND
Tel 01674-810356

PETSEARCH
Tel 0121-743-4133

THE POETRY SOCIETY
22 Betterton Street, London
WC2H 9BU.
Tel 0171-240-4810

RNIB
Mount Pleasant, Wembley,
Middlesex HA0 1RR.
Tel 0181-903-6666

ROYAL ASSOCIATION FOR DISABILITY AND REHABILITATION
12 City Forum, 250 City Road, London EC1V 8AF.
Tel 0171-250-3222

ROYAL HORTICULTURAL SOCIETY
PO Box 313, Vincent Square, London SW1P 2PE.
Tel 0171-834-4333

ROYAL SCOTTISH COUNTRY DANCE SOCIETY
12 Coates Crescent,
Edinburgh EH3 7AF.
Tel 0131-225-3854

ROYAL SOCIETY FOR ARTS
8 John Adam Street, London
WC2N 6EZ.
Tel 0171-930-5115

SCOTLAND'S GARDENS SCHEME
31 Castle Terrace, Edinburgh
EH1 2EL.
Tel 0131-229-1870

SOCIETY OF RECORDER PLAYERS
15 Palliser Road, London
W14 9EB.
Tel 0171-385-7321

THE WILDLIFE TRUSTS
The Green, Witham Park,
Waterside South, Lincoln
LN5 7JR.
Tel 01522-544400

WRITERS NEWS
PO Box 4, Nairn, Scotland
IV12 4H.
Tel 01667-454441;
Fax. 01667-454401

HELP LIST

Chapter 7: Helping In The Community

ACTION FOR SICK CHILDREN
Argyle House, 29-31 Euston Road, London NW1 2SD.
Tel 0171-833-2041

AGE CONCERN
Astral House, 1268 London Road, London SW16 4ER.
Tel 0181-679-8000
(in Wales, 4th Floor, 1 Cathedral Road, Cardiff, CF1 9SD. Tel 01222-371566; in Scotland 54A Fountainbridge, Edinburgh EH3 9PT. Tel 0131-228-5656; in Northern Ireland, 3 Lower Crescent, Belfast BT7 1NR. Tel 01232-245729).

ARTS COUNCIL (England)
14 St. Peter Street, London SW1P 3NQ.
Tel 0171-333-0100
(in Scotland, 12 Manor Place, Edinburgh EH3 7DD. Tel 0131-226-6051; in Wales, Holst House, Museum Place, Cardiff CF1 3NX. Tel 01222-394711; in Northern Ireland, 181 Stranmillis Road, Belfast BT9 5DU. Tel 01232-381591)

BARNARDO'S
Tanners Lane, Barkingside, Ilford, Essex IG6 1QG.
Tel 0181-550-8822

BIRMINGHAM DOGS HOME
New Bartholomew Street, Birmingham 5.
Tel 0121-643-5211

BRITISH BEEKEEPERS ASSOCIATION
National Agricultural Centre, Stoneleigh, Kenilworth, Warks CV8 2LZ.
Tel 01203-696679

BRITISH EXECUTIVE SERVICE OVERSEAS
164 Vauxhall Bridge Road, London SW1V 2RB.
Tel 0171-630-0644

BRITISH HEART FOUNDATION
14 Fitzhardinge Street, London W1H 4DH.
Tel 0171-935-0185

BRITISH RED CROSS
9 Grosvenor Crescent, London SW1X 7EJ.
Tel 0171-235-5454

MAKE THE MOST OF YOUR RETIREMENT

BRITISH TRUST FOR CONSERVATION VOLUNTEERS
36 St. Mary's Street, Wallingford, Oxon OX10 0EU.
Tel 01491-839766

BRITISH UNION FOR THE ABOLITION OF VIVISECTION
16a Crane Court, London N7 8LB.
Tel 0171-700-4888

BUSINESS IN THE COMMUNITY
8 Stratton Street, London W1X 5FD.
Tel 0171-629-1600

CANCER RESEARCH CAMPAIGN
10 Cambridge Terrace, London NW1 4JL.
Tel 0171-224-1333

CHICKENS LIB
PO Box 2, Holmfirth, Huddersfield HD7 1QT

THE CHILDREN'S SOCIETY
Edward Rudolf House, Margery Street, London WC1X 0JL.
Tel 0171-837-4299

COMMUNITY SERVICE VOLUNTEERS
237 Pentonville Road, London N1 9NJ.
Tel 0171-278-6601

CONTACT THE ELDERLY
15 Henrietta Street, Covent Garden, London WC2E 8QH.
Tel 0800-716543 (Freephone)

COUNCIL FOR BRITISH ARCHEOLOGY
Bowes Morrell House, 111 Walmgate, York YO1 2UA.
Tel 01904-671417

COUNCIL FOR THE PROTECTION OF RURAL ENGLAND
Warwick House, 25 Buckingham Palace Road, London SW1W 0PP.
Tel 0171-976-6433

FRIENDS OF THE EARTH
26-28 Underwood Street, London N1 7JQ.
Tel 0171-490-1555

GREENPEACE
Canonbury Villas, London N1 2PN.
Tel 0171-354-5100

HELP LIST

HELP THE AGED
St. James' Walk, London
EC1R 0BE.
Tel 0171-253-0253

HELP THE HOSPICES
34-44 Britannia Street,
London WC1X 9JG.
Tel 0171-278-5668

IMPERIAL CANCER RESEARCH FUND
PO Box 123, Lincoln's Inn Fields, London WC2A 3PX.
Tel 0171-242-0200

INTERNATIONAL VOLUNTARY SERVICE
Ceresole House, 53 Regent Road, Leicester LE1 6YL.
Tel 0116-2541862

LEONARD CHESHIRE FOUNDATION
Leonard Cheshire House, 26-29 Maunsel Street, London SW1P 2QN.
Tel 0171-828-1822

LYNX
PO Box 509, Dunmow, Essex CM6 1UH

THE MONKEY SANCTUARY
Looe, Cornwall.
Tel 015036-2532

NATIONAL ASSOCIATION FOR THE CARE AND RESETTLEMENT OF OFFENDERS
169 Clapham Road, London SW9 0PU.
Tel 0171-582-6500

NATIONAL ASSOCIATION OF LEAGUES OF HOSPITAL FRIENDS
2nd Floor, Fairfax House, Causton Road, Colchester, Essex CO1 1RJ.
Tel 01206-761227

NATIONAL ASSOCIATION FOR MENTAL HEALTH
Granta House, 15-19 Broadway, London E15 4BQ.
Tel 0181-519-2122

NATIONAL BACK PAIN ASSOCIATION
16 Elmtree Road, Teddington, Middlesex TW11 8ST.
Tel 0181-977-5474

NATIONAL CANINE DEFENCE LEAGUE
1 Pratt Mews, London NW1 0AD.
Tel 0171-388-0137

MAKE THE MOST OF YOUR RETIREMENT

NATIONAL TRUST
33 Sheep Street, Cirencester,
Gloucs. GL7 1QW.
Tel 01285-651818

PRO-DOGS
Rocky Bank, 4 New Road,
Ditton, Aylesford, Kent ME20
6AD.
Tel 01732-848499

JAMIESON, SCOTT AND PROWESS
118 Eaton Square, London
SW1.
Tel 0171-245-6153

PUBLIC APPOINTMENTS UNIT
Cabinet Office (OPSS), Horse
Guards Road, London SW1P
3AL.
Tel 0171-270-6210/17

RAMBLERS ASSOCIATION
1-5 Wandsworth Road,
London SW8 2XX.
Tel 0171-582-6878

REDWINGS HORSE SANCTUARY
Hill Top Farm, Hall Lane,
Frettenham, nr. Norwich,
Norfolk NR12 7LT.
Tel 01603-737432

RETIRED EXECUTIVES ACTION CLEARING HOUSE
Bear Wharf, 27 Bankside,
London SE1 9PD.
Tel 0171-928-0452

ROYAL NATIONAL INSTITUTE FOR THE BLIND
224 Great Portland Street,
London W1N 6AA.
Tel 0171-388-1266

ROYAL SOCIETY FOR THE PREVENTION OF CRUELTY TO ANIMALS
Causeway, Horsham, West
Sussex RH12 1HG.
Tel 01403-264181

THE SAMARITANS
10 The Grove, Slough, Berks.
SL1 1QP.
Tel 01753-532713

SAVE THE CHILDREN
Mary Datchelor House, 17
Grove Lane, London SE5
8RD.
Tel 0171-703-5400

SCOTTISH CONSERVATION PROJECTS TRUST
Ballan House, 24 Allen Park,
Stirling FK8 2QG.
Tel 01786-479697

HELP LIST

SKILLSHARE AFRICA
3 Belvoir Street, Leicester
LE1 6SL.
Tel 0116-2540517

SOCIETY FOR THE PROTECTION OF ANCIENT BUILDINGS
37 Spital Square, London E1 6DY.
Tel 0171-377-1644

3i's INDEPENDENT DIRECTOR PROGRAMME
91 Waterloo Road, London SE1 8XP.
Tel 0171-928-3131

UNITED NATIONS ASSOCIATION INTERNATIONAL SERVICE
Suite 3a, Hunter House, 57 Goodramgate, York YO1 2LS.
Tel 01904-647799

VICTIM SUPPORT
Cranmer House, 39 Brixton Road, London SW9 6DZ.
Tel 0171-735-9166

VOLUNTARY SERVICE OVERSEAS
317 Putney Bridge Road, Putney, London SW15 2PN.
Tel 0181-780-2266

WHALE AND DOLPHIN CONSERVATION SOCIETY
220 West Lea Road, Bath BA1 3RL.

WOMEN'S ROYAL VOLUNTARY SERVICE
234-244 Stockwell Road, London SW9 9SP.
Tel 0171-416-0146;
in Wales, 26 Cathedral Road, Cardiff CF1 9LJ. Tel 01222-28386; in Scotland, 19 Grosvenor Crescent, Edinburgh EH12 5EL. Tel 0131-337-2261

WOOD GREEN ANIMAL SHELTERS
Highway Cottage, Chishill Road, Heydon, Royston, Herts SG8 8PN.
Tel 01763-838329

YOUTH CLUBS UK
11 St. Bride Street, London EC4A 4AS.
Tel 0171-353-2366

Chapter 8: It's A Computer World

No list.

MAKE THE MOST OF YOUR RETIREMENT

Chapter 9: Taking A Break - Or Two!

ARP O50
See Chapter 1.

ATS TRAVEL
ATS House, 1 Tank Hill Road, Purfleet, Essex RM16 1SX.
Tel 01708-863198

ACCELERATED LEARNING SYSTEMS LTD
50 Aylesbury Road, Aston Clinton, Aylesbury, Bucks. HP22 5AH.
Tel 01296-631177

ACE STUDY TOURS
Babraham, Cambridge CB2 4AP.
Tel 01223-835055

ALLINGTON CASTLE
Maidstone, Kent ME16 0NB.
Tel 01622-54080

ALTERNATIVE TRAVEL GROUP LTD
Tel 01865-315678

ANGLERS WORLD HOLIDAYS
46 Knifesmithgate, Chesterfield, Derby S40 1RQ.
Tel 01246-221717
ANIMAL AUNTS
Tel 01428-712611

ARTHRITIS CARE
18 Stephenson Way, London NW1 2HD.
Tel 0171-916-1500

ARTSCAPE
Suite 4, Hamlet Court Business Centre, 18 Hamlet Court Road, Westcliff-on-Sea, Essex SS20 7LX.
Tel 01702-435990

ASSOCIATION OF BRITISH INSURERS
51 Gresham Street, London EC2V 7HQ.
Tel 0171-600-3333

BBC WORLDWIDE LTD
Freepost, Winterhill, Milton Keynes MK6 1HW.
Tel 01908-249177

THE BASKETMAKERS' ASSOCIATION
Threadgolds Farm, Great Braxsted, Witham, Essex CM8 3ER.
Tel 01621-891340

HELP LIST

BRITISH UNIVERSITIES ACCOMMODATION CONSORTIUM
Box 1526, University Park, Nottingham NG7 2RD.
Tel 0115-9504571

CAMPING AND CARAVANNING CLUB
Greenfields House, Westwood Way, Coventry CV4 8JH.
Tel 01203-694995

CAMPING FOR THE DISABLED
20 Burton Close, Dawley, Telford, Shrops.
Tel 01952-507653 (evenings)

CAMPUS HOTELS
PO Box 808, Edinburgh EH14 4AS.
Tel 0131-449-4034

CHOICE MAGAZINE
Apex House, Oundle Road, Peterborough PE2 9NP.
Tel 01733-555123

CHOICE MAGAZINE HOLIDAY CLUB
PO Box 155, Leicester LE1 9GZ.
Tel 0116-2513377

CONNECT
36 Collegiate Crescent, Sheffield S10 2BP.
Tel 0114-2683759

CO-OPERATIVE TRAVEL CARE
Tel 0161-827-1038

COSMOS HOLIDAYS
Tourama House, 17 Homesdale Road, Bromley, Kent BR2 9LX.
Tel 0181-464-3400

COUNTRYWIDE HOLIDAYS
Birch Heys, Cromwell Range, Manchester M14 6HU.
Tel 0161-225-1000

CRAFTS COUNCIL
44a Pentonville Road, Islington, London N1 9BY.
Tel 0171-278-7700

CYCLING FOR SOFTIES
2-4 Birch Polygon, Rusholme, Manchester M14 5HX.
Tel 0161-248-8282

EF INTERNATIONAL LANGUAGE SCHOOLS
5 Kensington Church Street, London W8 4LD.
Tel 0171-795-6675

MAKE THE MOST OF YOUR RETIREMENT

ENGLISH TOURIST BOARD
Thames Tower, Black's Road, London W6 9EL.
Tel 0181-846-9000

ENGLISH VINEYARDS ASSOCIATION
38 West Park, London SE9 4RH.
Tel 0181-857-0452

ENGLISH WANDERER
Tel 01740-653169

ENTENTE CORDIALE BUREAU
Dunstown, Mintlaw, Aberdeen AB4 7UJ.
Tel 0177-982249

EURO LANGUAGE SERVICES
PO Box 129, The Causeway, Worthing, BN12 6BP.
Tel 01903-506008

EUROCENTRES
56 Ecclestone Square, London SW1V 1PQ.
Tel 0171-233-9888

EUROGOLF
3b London Road, St. Albans, Herts. AL1 1LA.
Tel 01727-842256

FEATHERBED COUNTRY CLUB FOR DOGS
Tel 01494-711649

FIRST CHOICE HOLIDAYS
First Choice House, Peel Cross Road, Salford, Manchester M5 2AN.
Tel 0161-745-4633

GOETHE INSTITUTE
50 Princes Gate, Edinburgh Road, London SW7 2PH.
Tel 0171-411-3451

GREAT BRITISH GOLF
12 Sauterne Road, Prestwick, Scotland.
Tel 01292-678100

THE HEN HOUSE CLUB
Hawerby Hall, North Thoresby, Lincs. DN36 5QL.
Tel 01472-840278

HOLIDAY CARE SERVICE
2 Old Bank Chambers, Station Road, Horley, Surrey RH6 9HW.
Tel 01293-774535

HOME AND PET CARE
Tel 016974-78515

HELP LIST

HOME BASE HOLIDAYS
7 Park Avenue, London N13 5PG.
Tel 0181-886-8752

HOMESITTERS
Buckland Wharf, Buckland, Aylesbury, Bucks. HP22 5LQ.
Tel 01296-630730

HOUSEWATCH
Tel 01279-777412

INTERVAC
Intervac Home Exchange, 3 Orchard Court, North Wraxall, Wilts. SN14 7AD.
Tel 01225-892208

INTERVAL INTERNATIONAL LTD
Leaguestar House, Spring Gardens, Tinworth Street, London SE11 5EG.
Tel 0171-820-1515

THE IONA COMMUNITY
Iona, Argyll PA76 6SN.
Tel 016817-404

ITALIAN INSTITUTE
39 Belgrave Square, London SW1X 8NX.
Tel 0171-235-1461

JUST PEDALLING
9 Church Street, Coltishall, Norfolk NR12 7DW.
Tel 01603-737201

LAW SOCIETY
113 Chancery Lane, London WC2A 1PL.
Tel 0171-242-1222

MILLFIELD SCHOOL VILLAGE OF EDUCATION
Street, Somerset BA16 0YD.
Tel 01458-45823

ODYSSEY INTERNATIONAL
21 Cambridge Road, Waterbeach, Cambridge CB5 9NJ.
Tel 01223-861079

OLD RECTORY
Fittleworth, Pulborough, West Sussex RH20 1HU.
Tel 01798-82306

P & O CRUISES
77 New Oxford Street, London WC1A 1PP.
Tel 0171-831-1234

PARCEVALL HALL
Skyreholme, Skipton, North Yorks. BX23 6DG.
Tel 01675-672213

MAKE THE MOST OF YOUR RETIREMENT

PARKINSON'S DISEASE SOCIETY
22 Upper Woburn Place, London WC1H 0RA.
Tel 0171-383-3513

PLUSCARDEN ABBEY
Elgin, Grampian IV30 3UA.
Tel 0134-387257

PORTLAND HOLIDAYS
218 Great Portland Street, London W1N 5HG.
Tel 0171-388-5111

PRINCESS CRUISES
Tel 0171-800-2468
RCI LTD, Kettering Parkway, Kettering, Northants. NN15 6EY.
Tel 01536-310111

RAMBLERS HOLIDAYS LTD.
PO Box 43, Welwyn Garden, Herts. AL8 6PQ.
Tel 01707-331133

ROYAL NATIONAL INSTITUTE FOR THE BLIND
224 Great Portland Street, London W1N 6AA.
Tel 0171-388-1266

THE ROYAL SCHOOL OF NEEDLEWORK
Apartment 12a, Hampton Court Palace, East Molesey, Surrey KT8 9AY.
Tel 0181-943-1432

SAGA HOLIDAYS LTD (& SAGA MAGAZINE CLUB)
Saga Building, Freepost Folkestone, Kent CT20 1BR.
Tel 0800-300500 (Reservations); 0800-300456 (Brochures)

DAVID SCOTT INTERNATIONAL
Deerhurst House, Epping Road, Roydon, Harlow, Essex CM19 5RD.
Tel 01279-792162

SCOTTISH SPORTS COUNCIL
Caledonia House, South Gyle, Edinburgh EH12 9DQ.
Tel 0131-317-7200

SOLO'S HOLIDAYS LTD
Tel 0181-951-2800

SPANISH INSTITUTE
102 Eaton Square, London SW1.
Tel 0171-235-1484

HELP LIST

SPORTS COUNCIL
16 Upper Woburn Place,
London WC1H 0QP.
Tel 0171-388-1277

SUMMER MUSIC
22 Gresley Road, London
N19 3JZ.
Tel 0171-272-5664

THOMSON HOLIDAYS
Greater London House,
Hampstead Road, London
NW1 7SD.
Tel 0171-387-9321

THE TIMESHARE COUNCIL
23 Buckingham Gate,
London SW1E 6LB.
Tel 0171-821-8845

TRAFALGAR HOUSE
Europe Resorts Ltd.,
Goldsworth House, The
Goldsworth Park Centre,
Woking, Surrey GU21 3LF.
Tel 01483-747474

TRAVEL COMPANIONS (UK) LTD.
110 High Mount, Station
Road, London NW4 3ST.
Tel 0181-202-8478

UNIVERSAL AUNTS
PO Box 304, London SW4
0NN.
Tel 0171-738-8937

UNIVERSAL LANGUAGES
45 High Street, Kensington,
London W8 5EB.
Tel 0171-938-1225

VOYAGES JULES VERNE
21 Dorset Square, London
NW1 6QG.
Tel 0171-723-5066

MARTIN AND NINA WEATHERHEAD
Snail Trail Handweavers,
Penwenallt Farm, Cilgerran,
Cardigan, Dyfed.
Tel 01239-841228

WINE JOURNEYS
69-71 Banbury Road, Oxford
OX2 6PE.
Tel 01865-310244

WORLDWIDE HOME EXCHANGE CLUB
50 Hans Crescent, London
SW1X 0NA.
Tel 0171-823-9937

WORLD WINE TOURS LTD
Drayton St. Leonard,
Oxfordshire OX10 7BH.
Tel 01865-891919

MAKE THE MOST OF YOUR RETIREMENT

Chapter 10: Looking Back - And Looking Ahead

AGE CONCERN
Astral House, 1268 London Road, London SW16 4ER. Tel 0181-679-8000. (In Wales, 4th Floor, 1 Cathedral Road, Cardiff, CF1 9SD.
Tel 01222-371566;
in Scotland 54A Fountainbridge, Edinburgh EH3 9PT. Tel 0131-228-5656; in Northern Ireland, 3 Lower Crescent, Belfast BT7 1NR. Tel 01232-245729.)

ASSOCIATION OF RETIRED PERSONS
3rd Floor, Greencoat House, Francis Street, London SW1P 1DZ.
Tel 0171-828-0500

BRITISH ASSOCIATION FOR COUNSELLING
1 Regents Place, Rugby, Warks. CV21 2PJ.
Tel 01788-587328

CENTRAL COUNCIL FOR JEWISH COMMUNITY SERVICES
Stuart Young House, 221 Golders Green Road, London NW11 9DW.
Tel 0181-458-3282

CHARITIES AID FOUNDATION
Foundation House, Coach and Horses Passage, The Pantiles, Tunbridge Wells, Kent TN2 5TZ.
Tel 01892-512244

CO-OPERATIVE FUNERAL BOND
Freepost, London SE18 5B

COUNSEL AND CARE FOR THE ELDERLY
Twyman House, 16 Bonny Street, London NW1 9PG.
Tel 0171-485-1466 (10.30 a.m. to 4 p.m.)

CRUSE
Cruse House, 126 Sheen Road, Richmond, Surrey TW9 1UR.
Tel 0181-940-4818

DATEPLAN
0181-200-4945

HELP LIST

DIGNITY LTD.
Freepost, BM2415, Sutton Coldfield, West Midlands B72 1BR.
Tel 0800-269318 (Freephone)

FORCES HELP SOCIETY
122 Brompton Road, London SW3 1JE.
Tel 0171-589-3243

GOLDEN CHARTER
Freepost, London NW1 0YP.
Tel 0800-833800 (Freephone)

LAW SOCIETY
113 Chancery Lane, London WC2A 1PL.
Tel 0171-242-1222

MASS OBSERVATION ARCHIVE
University Library, University of Sussex, Brighton BN1 9QL. (Visits by appointment)

MATURE FRIENDS
Tel 0171-794-0208

NHS ORGAN DONOR REGISTER
Freepost BS 8793, PO Box 14, Patchway, Bristol BS12 6BR

NATIONAL ASSOCIATION OF BEREAVEMENT SERVICES
20 Norton Folgate, London E1 6DB.
Tel 0171-247-1080

NATIONAL ASSOCIATION OF CITIZENS ADVICE BUREAUX
115-123 Pentonville Road, London N1 9LZ.
Tel 0171-833-2181

NATIONAL ASSOCIATION OF FUNERAL DIRECTORS
618 Warwick Road, Solihull, West Midlands B91 1AA.
Tel 0121-709-0019

NATIONAL ASSOCIATION OF WIDOWS
54-57 Allison Street, Digbeth, Birmingham B5 5TH.
Tel 0121-643-8348

NORTHERN IRELAND ASSOCIATION FOR COUNSELLING
Bryson House, 28 Bedford Street, Belfast BT2 7FE.
Tel 01232-32583

MAKE THE MOST OF YOUR RETIREMENT

THE ORAL HISTORY SOCIETY
Department of Sociology,
University of Essex,
Wivenhoe Park, Colchester
CO4 3SQ

PET FUNERAL SERVICES
The Pet Cemetery, Brynford,
Holywell, Clwyd.
Tel 01352-710500

PILGRIM SERVICES
Alton Barnes, Marlborough,
Wilts. SN8 4JZ.
Tel 01672-851851

THE SOCIETY OF GENEALOGISTS
14 Charterhouse Buildings,
Goswell Road, London
EC1M 7BA.
Tel 0171-251-8799

TWO'S COMPANY
Tel 0171-409-0102

WAR WIDOWS ASSOCIATION OF GREAT BRITAIN
17 The Earls Croft, Coventry
CV3 5ES.
Tel 01203-503298

Index

Abroad 23, 31, 43, 59, 99, 168
Activities 143
Alcohol 93
Alternative medicine 67
Animals 127
Annuities 28
Arts 105, 125
Aspirin 198
Association of Retired Persons 26
Attendance allowance 65
Backs 72
Budgeting 39
Business 103
Business Angel 103
Calories 95
Capital gains 43
Carers 51
Centenarians 11
Charities 165
Charity shops 128
Cholesterol 89
Church 54
Collecting 106
Community help 117
Computers 130
Conservation 107, 126
Counselling 123
Crafts 108, 145
Crime prevention 22
Cruising 147
Culture 143
Dancing 108
Dieting 83, 94, 96
Disabled 116, 153
Drinks 92
Eating 84
Exercise 68
Expenditure 39
Family 47
Family trees 161
Fat 88
Fibre 84
Financial Advisers 25
Fish oil 98
Friends 52
Fruit 86
Funerals 166
Further education 104
GPs 64
Gardening 69, 109
Garlic 98
Gifts 164
Grandchildren 49
Handicapped 116, 153
Heart 73
Health 62, 154
Hearing 74
Help 123
Hire purchase 36
Hobbies 103
Holidays 141
Home exchanges 148
Home income plans 37
Hospital 61
Income 27, 37
Inheritance tax 43, 164
Insurance 154
Internet 136
Introduction agencies 170
Investments 32, 46

INDEX

ISAs 34
Joints, 71
Languages 151
Life policies 35
Lodgers 37
Medical care 65
Memories 158
Memory 75
Mortgages 36, 38
Moving 19
Music 110
National Insurance 38
Open University 104
Organ donation 166
Organic food 87
Overseas living 23, 59, 99,129
Painting 111
Partners 16, 48, 79, 169
Pen friends 55, 59
Pensions 28, 45
PEPs 34
Pets 112, 156
Phobias 80
Photography 113
Politics 124
Public appointments 124
Reading 113
Records 159
Relaxation 77
Rent-a-room scheme 37
Retreats 146
Safety 21
Saga 26
Salt 91
Security 155
Seminars 24
Sex 79

Sick, helping the 119
Sight 75
Singles 152
Sitters 156
Sleep 78
Solicitors 163
Smoking 81
Sport 69, 114
State benefits 29, 41
Stocks and shares 32
Stress 76
Sugar 90
Taxation 41, 43
Telephone 58
TESSAs 34
Time management 14
Timesharing 149
Tonics 97
Travelling 57
University of the 3rd Age 26
Vegetables 86
Visiting 56
Vitamins 97
Wine holidays 146
Wills 44, 162
Working 102
Writing 115
Young people 121

Help Yourself To A Job
Jackie Lewis ISBN 1-86144-033-2
£7.99 147 pp

Jackie Lewis's practical guide will give you the 'think smart' job-hunting skills you need to compete in today's tough market. She tackles head-on the special problems encountered by career-changers, or those already unemployed. Her simple activities will boost your confidence and get you thinking and moving towards your job goal right away. Jackie has helped hundreds of Job Club clients find the job they wanted using this creative person-centred approach.

Forget The Fear Of Food
Dr Christine Fenn ISBN 1-86144-035-9
£7.99 148 pp

Stop dieting and start living! A leading nutritionist explains why slimming diets don't work, and shows how developing self-esteem is the key to changing our eating habits. Packed with practical tips and activities to help you gain control over your eating and your life.

'A new approach . . . grab this book' *Dr Mary Cursiter*

Subfertility: A Caring Guide For Couples
Dr Phyllis Mortimer ISBN 1-86144-025-1
£7.99 104pp

Dr Mortimer gives a thorough and easy to understand explanation of the why, when and hows of conception, arming couples with the information they need to start looking at possible causes and solutions. She provides expert advice, encouragement and practical help to couples experiencing both major and minor fertility problems.

A Parent's Guide To Drugs
Judy Mackie ISBN 1-86144-028-6
£7.99 103 pp

Judy Mackie's no-nonsense guide addresses the questions about drugs that concern parents most, and arms them with the information they need to communicate effectively with their children. Whether you suspect your child, or their friends, may be taking drugs, or are simply worried by the horror stories and headlines - this practical guide will take you through the facts and basic steps, which you can use and develop to suit your own circumstances.

Education Matters
David Abbott ISBN 1-86144-029-4
£7.99 123 pp

Help yourself to some parent power and help your child get the most out of education. If you've ever felt confused by the new curriculum, or by school administration, don't be. Teacher David Abbott cuts through the jargon with straight facts and clear advice. Covers all you need to know, from what the Education Act means for your child, to how to check your child's real progress and talk to their teacher. Any parent can use this practical guide to help their child become a winner.

A Parent's Guide To Dyslexia And Other Learning Difficulties
Maria Chivers ISBN 1-86144-026-X
£7.99 123 pp

Many learning difficulties, once identified, can be overcome. If your child has, or you suspect they might have, learning difficulties, this essential guide gives you the facts you need to take action. It takes you step by step through diagnosis, treatment, education, and beyond into career options. Up-to-the minute facts and practical advice from the founder of the Swindon Dyslexia Centre, herself the mother of dyslexic sons.

Starting School
Lyn Carter ISBN 1-86144-031-6
£7.99 123 pp

Gives the information and advice you need to help your child to a happy and positive primary school experience. Shows how to plan for a good start, and suggests how to deal with problems that might come up. A good start to primary school lays the foundation for a successful education for your child. This book will help you create an enjoyable experience your child can build on in the future.

The Facts About The Menopause
Elliot Philipp ISBN 1-86144-034-0
£7.99 150 pp Pub Feb 98

Elliot Philipp, a consultant gynaecologist, answers the questions women most often ask about the menopause, its symptoms and treatments. He explains what the menopause is, evaluates HRT and alternative therapies, and offers practical advice on problems which can occur at this time.

This complete guide gives women the facts they need to approach their menopausal years with confidence.

Make The Most Of Being A Carer
Ann Whitfield ISBN 1-86144-036-7
£7.99 150 pp

If you are caring for someone with special needs, such as age, disability or ill-health, this is the guide you can turn to. Ann Whitfield, a social worker for many years, and herself a carer, offers expert, reliable and accessible advice covering the financial, legal, emotional and practical aspects of caring.

The problems of caring can be worrying, but they don't have to overwhelm you. This guide will point you to the help you need, and show you what you can do to better life for yourself and the person you care for.

Single Parent Power
Jackie Lewis ISBN 1-86144-038-3
£7.99 150 pp

A training and careers expert, herself a working single mother, explains how to make the most of government and other help available for lone parents. Shows how to plan for a career with prospects, and increase your earning power before going back to work. Details affordable childcare options, and tells how to build a social support network to help you keep going in emergencies. Whether you want to return to work in 5 weeks, 5 months, or 5 years, this is your guide to taking charge and making it happen the way you want.

Need2Know

Thank you for buying one of our books. We hope you found it an enjoyable read and a useful guide.
Need2Know produce a wide range of informative guides for people in difficult situations. Available in all good bookshops, or alternatively direct from:

Need2Know
1-2 Wainman Road
Woodston
Peterborough
PE2 7BU
Order Hotline: 01733 390801
Fax: 01733 230751

Titles

____	**Buying A House**	£5.99
____	**Stretch Your Money**	£4.99
____	**Breaking Up**	£5.99
____	**Superwoman**	£4.99
____	**Work For Yourself And Win**	£5.99
____	**The Expatriate Experience**	£6.99
____	**You And Your Tenancy**	£5.99
____	**Improving Your Lifestyle**	£5.99
____	**Safe As Houses**	£5.99
____	**The World's Your Oyster**	£5.99
____	**Everything You Need2Know About Sex**	£5.99
____	**Travel Without Tears**	£5.99
____	**Prime Time Mothers**	£5.99
____	**Parenting Teenagers**	£5.99

____	Planning Your Wedding	£5.99
____	Make A Success of Family Life	£4.99
____	Coping With Bereavement	£5.99
____	Get What You Pay for	£5.99
____	Take A Career Break	£4.99
____	Stress-Busting	£5.99
____	Subfertility	£7.99
____	A Parent's Guide to Drugs	£7.99
____	A Parent's Guide To Dyslexia And Other Learning Difficulties	£7.99
____	Starting School	£7.99
____	Education Matters	£7.99
____	Forget The Fear Of Food	£7.99
____	The Facts About The Menopause	£7.99
____	Help Yourself To A Job	£7.99
____	Make The Most Of Your Retirement	£7.99